GOD'S BEASTS

GOD'S BEASTS

**Identify and understand
animals in church carvings**

The stories that give point and purpose
to over one hundred varieties of animal and other figures
in our church carvings.

M.W.TISDALL

CHARLESFORT PRESS

ACKNOWLEDGEMENTS

My wife, Jenny, has been my support, my map reader and a very good one too, and at times my flash bearer. She has taken us to delightful churches in the quieter parts of small country villages and endured cold buildings in the winter months. I thank her very much for a real labour of love.

My local library and the chief librarian, Mrs Lancaster, have worked wonders with the systems to find rare and obscure books, or extracts from journals. Without their help and the Library service this enterprise would have been impossible. My eternal thanks to them.

Mrs Rita Wood, the wife of a Yorkshire vicar, has an uncanny knack of seeing the message in so many Norman or Romanesque carvings. I count myself lucky to have met her and thank her most warmly for all the advice she has given me.

The Folio Society published 'Bestiary' in 1992. This is a beautiful edition introduced by and translated from Bodleian Library M.S. Bodley 764 by Richard Barber. I thank them both for permission to use extracts in this book.

Line illustration drawings from the Book of Beasts. Trans T.H. White by permission of Jonathan Cape. Other line drawings by courtesy of Dover Publications.

The précis of the Harrowing of Hell is based on the 1924 translation by Mr. M.R. James of The Apocryphal New Testament; and is by permission of the Oxford University Press.

I am also grateful to Michael Bostick for the story of the Norse squirrel and to Loulou Brown for her help with the first steps in publishing.

I should like to record my thanks to the Dean and Chapter of the following cathedrals that have each given their permission for me to use the photographs that I took initially in pursuance of a hobby, for illustrations in this publication. Bristol, Exeter, Gloucester, Lincoln, Norwich, Hereford, Ripon, Worcester, Wells, Chester and Carlisle. I include also the Fellows of New College, Oxford; the priests in charge at several Minsters including Southwell, Beverley, Christchurch, Cartmel; and, too numerous to mention by name, the vicars and rectors of the many churches the length of this land.

Profits from the sale of this book will go to the Historic Churches Preservation Trust.

CONTENTS

INTRODUCTION

Are you intrigued by those curious carvings that we find inside and outside our churches? Do you ever wonder what they are and why they should be there? This book tries to answer some of these questions. It explores in the simplest terms the spiritual thought that lies behind items that most of us see as are mere decoration. In the process we shall rediscover many of the elements of Christian reasoning and some general moral truths.

The carvings were a text for the unlettered but not necessarily ignorant people of town and village. They also functioned as reminders to the monk or nun in their life away from the secular mainstream and who attended divine service frequently. Even in ordinary daily life most people certainly went to church every Sunday and many would have looked in everyday. They knew their Bible stories and many other stories from the relatively few books that were around; these include Aesop's fables, the Reynard romances, the Arthurian legends and the stories about animals in a book called the Bestiary. I shall refer frequently to the Bestiary because it was probably the most well known book after the Bible and it is the source for nearly all the information on animal lore that was available to preacher and layman alike. We should also remember that Christianity throughout western Europe was a uniform whole with the same books and the same ideas. So the carvings are also very similar throughout. We find that we can enjoy similar items containing the same messages whether we are in Scotland or the South of Italy.

The theology and philosophy of the time held that since man had been created in God's image he must be the 'highest' of the animals. The rest of creation was for Man's instruction and enjoyment. If nature was for our instruction then attached to each animal there must be some direction that would improve our understanding. The Bestiary is a collection of such instructions that started with relatively few animals in a book called the Physiologus. This was written in Alexandria in the early centuries AD. It expanded significantly in the 11th and 12th centuries and it is the illustrations from those books that form the basis for many of the designs in church carvings. In the 13th and 14th centuries there were some more sources such as the major encyclopaedias called 'Speculae' or 'Mirrors' to the natural world. There were also Books of Hours, beautifully illustrated, for the rich and devout. The carvers therefore had many pictures to which to turn when the patron said that he wanted this or that as a constituent of his theme in the church. The battle between good and evil, between God and Satan, or Man and his conscience form a significant proportion of the spiritual themes in church carving. There are also many illustrations of Bible scenes and very many occasions when an animal story known to everyone illustrates by way of metaphor a whole doctrinal truth. It is easier to remember a picture than to get one's mind round relatively complicated notions like 'Salvation' or 'Redemption'. For instance both the Elephant and the Salamander tell us something about baptism; the Antelope about the dangers of drink. The Crocodile and Hydrus or Samson rending the Lion's jaws tell us about delivery from the power of sin.

these matched stories; many designs have their origin there.

Animal carvings are important for the message that they carry. They never pretend to be true to nature pictures. *The carvings are there not to tell us about the physical nature of the animal but to tell us a moral or spiritual truth about ourselves.* It really does not matter even if the animal is one we now know does not exist. To them a griffin or a unicorn was just as real as an elephant or a tiger. There was no need to be concerned about the strict 'scientific' truth. We demean ourselves when we belittle them for their lack of knowledge. If we do not know the story then it is we who are to be pitied.

I should like to have included a picture from a Bestiary for every animal under discussion. That would have made the book very cumbersome and possibly too scholarly for those who I hope will enjoy it. Please trust that there is a Bestiary somewhere with a picture that would make a suitable source unless I state otherwise and explain that I am making an intelligent guess, not a well backed statement.

The writers of the Bestiaries do indulge in sermonising as they make the spiritual or moral point to the story. We are usually more reserved on these matters and the descriptions may grate on the modern ear. We shall be more tolerant of their situation if we acknowledge that they were talking about the full range of human frailty and experience.

The difficult part is deciding the nature of the figure that we might remember from a chance visit to a church. There is a list of 'short cuts' at the end of the book that

Every carving carries some message. Some of the messages would be offensive if the Church tried to convey them in the same way today. We may not know or understand all of them but we shall miss so much if all that we can admire is the skill of the carver and the beauty of the wood or stone.

Some of the carvings of the 15th and 16th centuries refer to the social and political abuses of their day and so would often have two meanings. People seem to have had little difficulty in accommodating to variety in shades of understanding.

Theologians saw in the Old Testament many episodes that seemed to presage events in the New. They put these parallel events together calling the Old Testament one the Type and the New Testament one the Antitype. A famous book called the Biblia Pauperum collected and illustrated should help you to find the right section. From there move around as curiosity invites. The book does not progress except in alphabetical sequence but some of the items will often be relevant to several others so do read all even if not in a single session. It is only then that you will appreciate the range and depth of the spiritual messages that the carvings have to tell us. Treat it as you would a flora where a quick scan through identifies flowers that are obviously like one another and where further search should concentrate.

I have expanded a little from the strict domain that the title implies because allied themes appear so often that it seems an oversight to pass them by without comment or clarification.

We would all like just one answer or one meaning to every question about a carving but religious symbolism has too many facets for such an easy outcome. Instead we should join M.D.Anderson who points out that 'To assume certainty is to court disillusion, but to weigh possible alternatives is to achieve a richer understanding.'

At the end is a Bibliography that contains those books mentioned in the text, plus some others that make good general background reading. I also give a list of what I have called 'Concepts'; the abstractions or notions that are implicit in the theological or philosophical points that the Church discusses.

In each 'chapter' I have given the animal under discussion a capital letter at the beginning of the name purely so that if you are looking through quickly, you will be able to pick out the most important items without trouble.

Some animals wear a crown round their necks in which case they are said to be 'gorged.' This means that they have a heraldic significance, such as being the badge of a great lord, but they have no spiritual purpose.

In some places I have used theological terms such as 'Baptism' in a very broad generic sense and do not wish to imply automatic or magical access to a spiritual life.

Finally there some Notes at the end for the more academically inclined. They discuss possible new insights into the understanding of some of the carvings, and some make what I hope are interesting asides to the main themes.

Ask the beasts and they shall teach thee; and the fowls of the air, and they shall tell thee.

Job 12;7.

The visible world teaches us things concerning the invisible, the earth contains images of heavenly things; in order that by means of these lower objects we may mount up to that which is above. As God made man in his own image and after his own likeness, so he created lower animals after the likeness of heavenly prototypes.

Origen.

To assume certainty is to court disillusion, but to weigh possible alternatives is to achieve a richer understanding.

M.D.Anderson in Imagery of British Churches.

It is not possible to ascend into contemplating heavenly hierarchies if our wit be not led by some material thing.

Bartholomeus Anglicus in De Proprietatibus Rerum.

AGNUS DEI

'Agnus Dei qui tollis peccata mundi'
Behold the Lamb of God who takes away the sin of the world.
Jn 1:29

John the Baptist's great pronouncement is so central to the Christian faith, that this book shall begin with it, just as so many churches carry this emblem over their entrance way. I have written more about Sheep and Lambs under Sheep

This particular Lamb is always shown with a bent foreleg supporting the Vexillum or flag of victory; in this case Victory over sin

2. Hilfield. Dorset.
The Lamb sheds blood for Mankind.

1. Alford. Som.
The Lamb with the Vexillum, the flag of victory.

and death. It would have a red cross of the Resurrection on a white ground.

Sometimes we find the Lamb with blood spurting into a communion cup; thus emphasising the redeeming blood of Christ and so linking the resurrection with our redemption.

AMPHISBAENA

A mouthful of a word, but the only one we have to describe a dragon or serpent with a head at both ends, and carvings of which adorn many of our churches. Two fierce heads are obviously better than one. It could coil into a hoop with one head grasped by the other, and thus roll backwards or forwards. It is therefore a suitable example of deceit such as that shown by individuals who live a double life. They often describe Satan as the Arch Deceiver and double headed forms are one of his many manifestations.

This is taken further on a misericord at Worcester where a female head has the cloven feet of the devil. Peeping from

4. Swavesey. Cambridge.
On his back because defeated but still alert.

3. Worcester Cathedral.
The 'deceitfulness of women.'

behind harpy like wings, is another female head. This is a nicely condensed essay on the alleged deceitfulness of women.

Just occasionally the Amphisbaena may have a positive connotation, for according to the Bestiary it had eyes like lamps and only one head slept at a time. It could therefore be an example of Vigilance; but I confess I do not know of such an example in English church carvings. There may be one at Sauve Majeur, Gironde, where a twin headed serpent looking remarkably alert keeps watch from the apse at the east end, a position where we often find other figures watching for the second coming. (c.f. Horse.)

5. Luppitt. Devon.
Christ as Centaur attacks the Arch-deceiver.

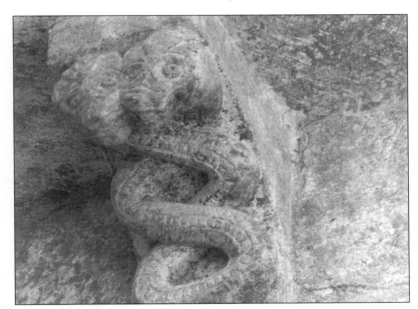

6. La Sauve Majeur. Gironde, Fr.
Alert for the Second Coming

7. Withersfield. Suff.
An evil head at either end.

AN ANGEL WITH A BOOK

In association with a Lion, a Bull and an Eagle, each of which may have wings, we may often find what looks like an Angel holding a book. This is St Matthew. Out of deference and in order to distinguish him from lesser saints, he is usually shown winged and holding a scroll or a book. This makes one think that he is an angel but almost certainly nearby will be representations of the other three also holding a scroll and bearing wings. See under Tetramorph for the origins of these symbols.

8. Castle Frome. Font. H&W.
St Matthew

9. Brent Knoll. Som.
St Matthew with a scroll.

ANTELOPE

We recognise the Antelope by his very serrated horns. These bear little resemblance to those of a modern Antelope but are *the* important part of his description in the Bestiary. This Antelope was speedy and agile and could saw down trees with these sharp horns. One day it went down to the river to drink and afterwards teased the bushes with his horns to such an extent that they became entangled. The hunter (Satan) then came and killed it.

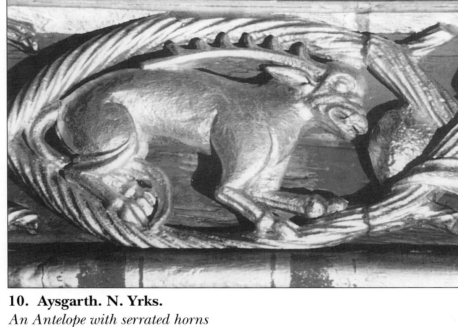

10. Aysgarth. N. Yrks.
An Antelope with serrated horns

The two horns represent the Old and New Testaments; with these any individual should be able to saw off all vices; pride, avarice, adultery, etc., that in the story are represented by this undergrowth. However having partaken of the demon drink (the river is figuratively a resource for alcohol), the Old and New Testaments become useless to him so that he indulges in all sorts of immoral pursuits. He is now the Devil's person. One writer puts it so charmingly, 'It is pleasant to be under the shadow of the bush, rich foods, fine drinks, beautiful women, beautiful clothes, palfreys ambling and fat, gold and silver, and money which does much harm to him amassing it.'

So an Antelope is a warning that proud though we might be of our knowledge of the Bible there is always danger. Sins such as gluttony and drink may make us foolish in the extreme. We should not squander the guidance available to us.

Some Antelopes appear with a crown worn as a necklet. This is a Heraldic Antelope for it was the badge of several kings and dukes, not least Henry V; it is said to be 'gorged.' It is often even less realistic than the truer antelopes and carries no moral meaning.

11. Ripon. N. Yrks.
A pair of Antelopes to remind us of the dangers that lie in dissolute pursuits

12. Kings Lynn. Norf. St Nicholas.
The heraldic Antelope; also dangerously proud.

13. Faversham. Kent.
A good Christian holding to Biblical teaching ?

APE

The Ape we observe in church carvings is not the playful monkey that medieval entertainers kept with them to entertain the crowds. Some simian carvings are of monkeys but the Bestiary writer includes them all under the heading, 'Ape' and it is the Ape that has a lesson for us.

These writers point out that the Ape has no cauda (tail), in much the same way as the Devil has no codex (law). So by the happy congruence of their dog Latin and the sounds of the words, in fact a Medieval pun, they made the Ape equivalent to the devil,

15. Forrabury nr. Boscastle, Cornwall.
A warning about licentiousness.

14. Earl Soham. Suffolk
A debased relation of Man.

who is outside the Law.

Additionally they point out that Man was made a little lower than the angels. Heb 2:7. Ps.8:5. Man therefore was a poor relation of the angels, so the Ape, because he looks like a person but clearly is not, must be a debased relation of Man. He pretended to have but was unworthy of, human status. He was a trickster, a sycophant, a hypocrite, cowardly, lecherous and particularly ugly.

He came from 'Egypt' that region often used as an example of the sinful life from

17

which Man had to be saved by Christ.

He was addicted to sex. Thus an Ape exposing the buttocks, at Forrabury near Boscastle, may well warn of licentiousness. A naked woman leading Apes into the jaws of hell, as at Bristol, refers to a story about a woman with nine children but no husband who is given a penance by Christ that, 'hereafter she will lead apes in Hell.' This association of apes and women was popularly applied to old maids or to wives who refused their husbands their conjugal rights. They would pay in eternity by being tied to a band of the most lecherous creatures imaginable. (Note 1)

16. Bristol Cathedral.
A Maid leads apes into hell.

An Ape in chains is a person addicted to the pleasures of this world.

An Ape with a urinal is a parody on the medical profession. Doctors, who made many of their diagnoses by the colour, taste (diabetes) and no doubt, smell, of the urine; were not held in high esteem at the time. At Beverley St Mary the Ape is being offered or demanding a very large fee in coin form.

Apes get up to tricks. They play pipes, flutes and other instruments that make a 'devilish' noise; some of the many diversions of which the Church disapproves at this time.

We will often find an Ape tending to, or in competition with, a fox. They were usually friends, both outside the law, in the popular stories of the day about Reynard and his friends. (The Brer Rabbit stories fulfil much the same slot nowadays.)

So, the playful chimp that we have learned to enjoy and tolerate is far removed from this persona of Satan's alter ego of the Middle Ages.

17. Beverly St Mary. ER. Yrks.
The greedy physician.

18. Faversham. Kent.
In chains to sin.

19. St Columb Major. Corn.
A pair of Apes making devilish music.

19

ASP

An Asp is a snake or small dragon that has one large ear pressed to the ground and the other blocked or about to be blocked by its tail.

The Asp was a famous serpent which was why Shakespeare used it for the snake that killed Cleopatra and it is probably the only variety about which many of us have heard.

The Asp of the Bestiaries is one of the many adders, snakes and vipers that all lie in wait to bring people to a horrible death. Because it blocks its ears and resists the powers of the snake charmer, the writers make the parallel with people of this world who stop up one ear with the desires of the world. The other ear they block with sin in

20. Egloskerry. Cornwall.
An Asp on the north tympanum, the Devil's side.

order not to hear the voice of the Lord.

One faces a basilisk at Exeter. Another is on a tympanum at Egloskerry. In other places where we find carvings of serpent or dragon forms with large ears, we may guess that they are meant to be Asps.

The (Vulgate) Bible mentions the Asp in Ps 91:13. 'Thou shalt tread upon the Asp and the Basilisk', and points to the intentional deafness in Ps 58.4. 'The wicked ...are like the deaf adder which stoppeth the ear.' The medieval equivalent of our modern adage 'There is none so deaf as those that will not hear.'

21. Exeter Cathedral.
A pair of evildoers. An Asp on the Lt. faces a Basilisk on the Rt.

ASPIDOCHELONE, a variety of Whale

The Greeks had used this word for the large shield shaped turtle and also for any sea animal like a whale. The Bestiary writers use this same word to describe an enormous sea monster that has the following two stories attached to it.

(One) It was so big that sailors might mistake it for an island with sand, grass and trees growing on its back. The unwise would land and light a fire. The heat would waken the 'whale' that dived taking ship and sailors to the bottom.

The Bestiary tells us that the same fate will befall those who know nothing of the wiles of the Devil; 'they will plunge into the fires of Gehenna with him.'

(Two) The Aspidochelone also had very sweet breath that it used to lure little fish into its mouth and then swallow them. The bigger fish had learned wisdom and avoided this fate.

'The same end awaits those who are not

22. Earl Soham. Suff.
The incautious taken by the devil.

23. Queen Camel. Somerset.
Unwise sailors moor alongside.

firm in their faith and yield to all temptations.'

This second story is the one that we usually see. A big fish swallows a lesser fish. It is easy to carve and easy to make the subject fit any convenient corner of the design

The ship and sailor's story are rarely seen in carving but there are examples at Alne and Queen Camel

The Medieval writer points out that innocence and trust are not enough. We need the wisdom of the Lord to avoid such a terrible outcome.

24. Lakenheath. Suff.
The unwary (little fish) taken by the devil (big fish).

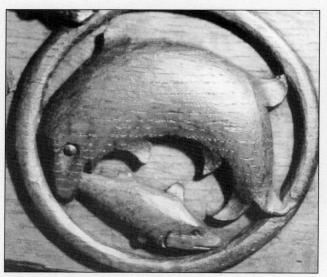

25. Beverly Minster. E.R.Yrks.
The heedless taken by the devil

26. Kidlington. Oxon.
The thoughtless taken by the devil.

27. Alne. N. Yrks.
Unwise sailors remind us of our own unwise actions

Ass

The Ass with the Ox at the manger is the only modern instance of an Ass in some sort of church setting. It has achieved great popularity in spite of not being mentioned in the Biblical accounts.

The Ass of Bestiary and Bible has both good and bad connotations. The males have notable physical endowments. Ezek.23:20 'For she doted on her paramours, whose flesh is like the flesh of asses', and so we find them associates of Lechery. (Note 7). Criminals and adulterers in the middle ages were made to ride through the streets on an Ass, naked and

28. Gloucester Cathedral.
The Aesop fable of the Ass and the Lap Dog.

facing backwards.

The Ass was an honourable mount in Christ's time. The idea that it was a particularly lowly creature came later with the emphasis by preachers on Christ's humility. The nobility of the Ass may be the important factor in the story of the triumphal entry into Jerusalem, and the Messiah was expected to arrive riding on an Ass. Zech 9:9. Mary, later to be Queen of Heaven, also rides an Ass to Bethlehem and on her flight into Egypt.

The Feast of Asses, later known as the Feast of Fools was first celebrated when the Church included the 'Flight into Egypt' into the

29. Hereford Cathedral.
The reprobate going nowhere fast. He rides a horse but it illustrates the point.

Christmas liturgy. It later degenerated and became a repulsive burlesque of the most sacred Church matters, so much so that in the 13th century the Church suppressed it.

We think of Asses as being fairly stupid and this is how we talk of them just as they did in the Middle Ages. We find many jesters and fools with Asses ears and sometimes even whole head-dresses, much as they must have appeared in their miracle plays. Asses' ears make for a convenient shorthand to describe wilful foolishness. For instance, There is none so blind as those that will not see; like the 'fool' with eyes shut at Christchurch.

We also find the Ass in Aesop's fable of the Ass and the Lapdog at Gloucester. The hard worked Ass is jealous of the soft life and pampering bestowed upon the lapdog. One day he breaks his tethers, gallops into the

30. Christchurch Priory. Dorset.
A 'Fool' with asses ears and his eyes shut. Possibly; 'There's none so blind as those that will not see...'

master's house, frisks and kicks as he has seen the dog do, in the process causing immense damage. He ends by placing his front legs on his master in the same way as the dog does, so knocking him to the ground. As a reward he is taken away and beaten to within an inch of his life. 'Oh why was I not satisfied with the work, good food and shelter that my master provided for me.'

His sins are those of jealousy and presumption.

The moral 'Be content with one's lot and do not be jealous of the apparent idleness of others.'

It may also help to know the story of Balaam and his Ass, which, though I have not seen it in carvings in England, probably appears somewhere because it carries a lesson. It certainly appears in France. Balaam goes off on an errand against God's express wishes. So God sends an angel to bar the way. This angel is

31. Aston Eyre. Shrops. Tympanum.
The entry into Jerusalem.

visible to the Ass but not initially to Balaam, and he vents his anger on the poor old Ass, his otherwise trusty friend. Ultimately he does see the angel and he does feel remorse. Num. 22.This story figures in Medieval plays to give Biblical authority to the need for penance and contrition.

The picture of an Ass with a harp is surprisingly common on Norman and early gothic churches. It refers to a story about Boethius' ass, in a fable of Phaedrus', widely current in the Middle Ages. A monk or cleric is admonished 'Are you like an Ass listening to a harp (or lyre)?' Here the Ass is pretending to like the music by wagging his ears in appreciation. Unfortunately he has no significant understanding of the music, just as the admonished person has no spiritual understanding. In an extension of this line of thinking the Ass came to be seen as an example of laziness, especially spiritual laziness. The Ass with the lyre was a reproof to those who wasted their time and their talents. Other animal musicians indulging in very human but unspiritual activity could also be seen as examples of the potential for grace of an all powerful God.[1]

[1]. Ref 10. p57.

32. Chartres Cathedral. Eure et Loir.
Spiritual idleness and incomprehension as in Phaedrus' fable.

33. Wells Cathedral.
The Devil is really only a fool.

BASILISK AND COCKATRICE

We can recognise these in carvings for they have the cockscomb and wings of the cock plus a serpent's tail, though it is easy to mistake them for just another grotesque based on a cock.

The Basilisk was born in a dung hill, from the egg of a seven year old cock, hatched by a toad. From such confused beginnings it is not surprising to find Basilisks evolving into and merging with the Cockatrice by the 14th Century. The terms are now synonymous.

The important part of the Basilisk story is that it bears a lethal glance. If it sees you before you see it, then you are a dead person. The

34. Stonham Aspal. Suff.
Basilisk with an Amphisbaena tail. Two sorts of evil in one body.

only protection was to carry a mirror or crystal sphere with which to reflect back the glance. Otherwise only a cock or a weasel armed with rue could face it unharmed.

Symbolically the crystal sphere is equivalent to the Virgin Mary; the vessel that God chose to protect Christ from Satan's power.

As with the Asp, the Basilisk was one of Satan's many forms. Ps

35. Worcester Cathedral.
A Weasel armed with rue fearlessly faces a Basilisk.

91:13. 'Thou shalt tread upon the Asp and the Basilisk.' (Vulg)

Later, the glance of the Basilisk was equated with the unchaste look from the harlot; and with the covetous eye that could be cast at a pretty woman.

So the Basilisk can symbolise lust, and sometimes pride, and remind us of yet another form for the Evil One. Indirectly it may have reminded those who called upon the Virgin Mary that they might ask her to use her power to help them resist evil.

36. Astley. Warw.
A Basilisk.

37. Beverley Minst. E.R.Yrks.
Evil in all its glory.

38. Denston. Suff.
A Cockatrice.

27

BAT

It is usually easy to identify bats in carvings but a few are difficult and with some the identification is uncertain. (Ault Hucknall. Fig.41)

By the very nature of their lifestyle bats have for long been associated with the works of darkness. The bats on misericords, bench ends and roof bosses are often true 'bats out of hell.'

Medieval preachers extended the metaphor, pointing out that bats have feeble eyes and wings made of leather. They tell us that the 'humour' in their eye that

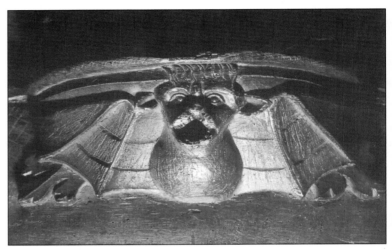

39. Christchurch Priory. Dorset.
A Bat out of Hell.

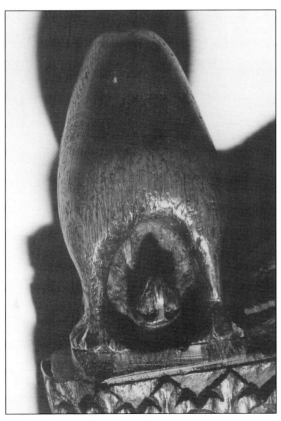

40. Earl Soham. Suff.
A Bat hanging upside down?

should have made them big passes into their wings, so they are small. So, 'for their flying they have lost their sight.' This would imply that the preachers thought that they should be much larger animals content with a land bound existence. They have committed the sin that we might call presumption by venturing into spheres for which they were not designed.[2] (Doctors still use the medieval word 'humour' to describe the contents of the eye.)

We are thankful, therefore, to find that Bats can also symbolise better things. The Bestiary tells us 'they hang on to each other alternately, and depend from any place like a bunch of grapes. If one lets go, they would all be scattered. 'And this they do from a certain duty of affection, of a kind which is difficult to find in man.' Bats exhibiting this co-operative behaviour point to the advantages to be obtained by staying within Holy Church.

[2]. Ref 49. p199.

41. Ault Hucknall. Derbys.
Two Bats?, on chancel arch

42. Romsey Abbey. Hants.
A Bat on a North side corbel.

43. Dunblane Cathedral.
The Sin of Presumption?

BEAR

The Bear was well known to people in the Middle ages. In the sport of Bear baiting he was attacked by dogs and also he was exhibited as a performing animal.

A Bear on the loose must have been a frightening encounter. So it is appropriate that the muzzled Bear tells us about having our desires under control.

In early Medieval times they thought that Bears copulated face to face like humans and by the 12th century the Bear was an accepted symbol of male

44. Tickencote. Rutl.
Muzzled to show that desire is under control.

45. Barton-le-Street. N.Yrks. Font.
Sin in chains now that Christianity is in charge.

fornication. Luxuria (lust) may ride a Bear in pictures of the Seven Deadly Sins.

The writers of the Bestiaries knew that Bears were born only a few weeks after conception. They state that they look like formless lumps of flesh and that the Mother then has to lick them into shape. (This is the origin for our modern phrase.) The moral point is that the inborn forces of nature can be brought to perfection by instruction, specifically Christian instruction in a Church context. It ties in well with the story of the muzzled Bear.

The Bear's well known liking for honey features in a Reynard story. Here Reynard cons Bruin into looking for honey in a split open tree, but the split is only held by wedges. When Bruin has his head in, Reynard knocks out the wedges and catches him. 'Thus the Devil catches those who pursue too avidly the sweet things of life.'

There are two other points to remember about the Bear. He licks his lips when contemplating favourite morsels; as does the glutton.

Bears like honey and will lick away the bees to obtain it. So the glutton wastes the fruit of other's labours.[3]

[3]. Ref 49. p495.

46. Bristol Cathedral.
A Bear with his head in a cleft tree. 'Trapped by an addiction to the sweet things in life.'

47. Gt. Doddington. N'hants.
A muzzled Bear.

48. Earl Soham. Suff.
A Bear tied to a post ; 'under control.'

BEAVER

It is rare to find accurate pictures of Beavers. Lakenheath and Wilton (Hockwold cum Wilton) have the best. The Bestiaries have pictures that look very like dogs or even cats probably because the description is lacking in detail and live Beavers came from far away. The illustrators concentrate on the story, see below, and the pose that they demonstrate is one we tend to interpret as a dog or a cat attending to the toilet of the nether regions.

Beavers, like the Civet and some other mammals, produce a scent from glands around the anus that scent manufacturers prize highly. The Bestiary writers thought that it was the testicles that were the necessary organs. Hence the story in the Bestiary of the hunted Beaver who will bite off his testicles and throw them to the hunter. The next time they hunt him

49. Wilton (Hockwold cum Wilton). Norf.
A Beaver bites off his testicles. The saint can more single mindedly follow the spiritual life.

he can rear up on his hind legs to exhibit his now eunuch like condition and thus evade further molestation.

The animal at Bristol may be a Beaver about to castrate itself rather than a cat or a dog. In the same way the Beaver from Les Andelys, France, is about to castrate itself. Compare it with the picture of the rather cat-like dog from the same church; Fig.120. Dogs heal by licking and this is one of their characteristic poses in Bestiary lore.

The symbol is therefore of the saint who would cut himself off from the flesh and the desires of the flesh; the more single-mindedly to follow the spiritual life. By an extension of this theme the Beaver becomes a symbol of chastity.

50. Les Andelys. Eure. Fr.
A Beaver prepares to bite off his testicles. c.f. Fig.120. p.64.

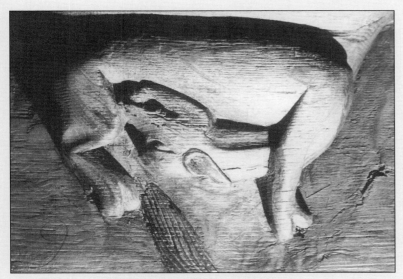

51. Solignac. Haute Vienne. Fr.
Beaver like activity.

52. Bristol Cathedral.
Probably a Beaver turning to castrate himself.

53. Beverley Minster. E.R.Yrks.
Misericord supporter. A Beaver about to castrate himself.

BIRD IN THE VINE

This is very common and usually delightfully and beautifully carved.

'I am the true vine and my father is the husbandman...as the branch cannot bear fruit of itself, except it abide in me, no more can ye except ye abide in me...He that abideth in me and I in him, the same bringeth forth much fruit.' Jn.15:1

'The Kingdom of Heaven is like unto a grain of mustard seed...which, when it is grown becomes a tree, so that birds of the air come and lodge in the branches thereof.' Mat.13:31

54. Crowcombe. Som.
Christian souls safe in Christ.

55. Monkleigh. Devon.
Souls secure from want.

The quotations tell us about the origin of this Christian doctrine. They highlight the thoughts behind the carvings. The picture is universal and beautifully formed on rood screen, capital and doorway. The Bird in the vine is the Christian Soul 'in Christ', safe and spiritually secure.

BOAR and also see Pig

We recognise Boars by the little tusks protruding from the jaw.

Boars carry evil connotations. This association with matters malevolent was maintained in all sorts of ways and for many hundreds of years. Clement of Alexandria in explaining why Moses forbade the eating of pork, associated the animal with boundless lust, greed and aggressiveness, and these negative attributes continued into the Middle Ages. When they portrayed the Seven Deadly Sins in the plays and processions of the Middle Ages, the Boar was the mount for gluttony. It is also an attribute of sloth.

The hunter chasing the Boar is often symbolic. It is tempting to think that it is just a picture of a not uncommon and rather exciting activity. However in a church it carries a meaning. The hunter is the priest who must destroy sin, exemplified by the

56. Stowlangtoft. Suff.
Quietly but thoroughly evil.

57. Beverley St Mary. E.R.Yrks.
A Christian knight tackles the evil boar.

Boar. In the baptismal service we renounce the Devil and all his works. So it is appropriate that we should find the Boar hunt on fonts.

Boars with tusks and of fearsome aspect represent 'the cruel princes of this world'.

Of course 'the cruel princes' never see themselves in this light. Maybe we are being told that there is something of the cruel prince in all our natures.

58. Astley. Warw.
'A Prince of this world.'

59. St Marychurch. Torquay. Devon. Font.
Renouncing the Devil and all his works.

WINGED BULL and see Ox

The winged bull is the emblem of St Luke.

There are several strands to the story of how the four Evangelists arrive at their symbols.   See Ez 10:14, Ez 1:5-14; Rev 4:6-8 'And round about the throne were four beasts..., the first beast was like a lion, the second beast like a calf, the third beast has the face of a man, the fourth beast was like a flying eagle.'

Medieval commentators noted how Luke's gospel begins with the story of the sacrifice by Zacharias the priest. Luke 1:8. The Ox was a sacrificial animal and one that Zacharias might have had to sacrifice from time to time. So the Ox or Calf or Bull became associated with St Luke and is one of the four figures of the Tetramorph.

60. Poughill. Corn.
A winged Bull well copied by the carver from a very inadequate original.

61. Faversham. Kent.
The emblem of St Luke.

37

62. Avington. Berks.

Not winged but at the east end of a church dedicated to St Luke and St Mark.

63. Hilfield. Dorset.

St Luke writer and painter.

64. Brent Knoll. Som.

St Luke with his scroll.

CAMEL

The Camel's hump makes it fairly easy to recognise although some have just a mop like rosette instead of a true fleshy hump.

Humility, that most Christlike of expressions, the very antithesis of pomp, vainglory, pride, power and self seeking, surely has an exemplar for us from the animal kingdom. It is the Camel who kneels to take on his burden. In the same way Christ humbled himself to take on the sin of the whole world. It is in this sense that we find the Camel in most of the bench end and misericord carvings.

The Camel is also Prudent

65. Boston. Lincs.
A Camel kneels in humility.

66. Brent Knoll. Som.
A Camel as Christ ready to take on the burden of the sin of the world.

because it takes on water to forestall future needs.

On the negative side the female camel was (mistakenly) famous for her desire and enjoyment of prolonged sexual intercourse. Hence she came to be a metaphor for a prostitute and 'Luxuria', the unchaste state. Jer.2:20-24 'You (Israel) bowed down to the harlot...know what you have done, a restive young camel interlacing her tracks...in her heat sniffing the wind, who can restrain her lust?'

The Bestiary reminds

us of Matt 19:24. 'It is easier for a Camel to go through the eye of a needle than it is for a rich man to enter the Kingdom of god.' It then interprets this, saying that it is easier for Christ to suffer for those who love the things of this world than for such individuals to be converted to Christ. This highlights the degree of humility that Christ showed on behalf of all conditions of humanity.

Dromedary

The Bestiary distinguishes between Camel and Dromedary. The Dromedary was smaller and could run much faster, one hundred miles in a day. The Bestiary illustrators and therefore the carvers do not distinguish between one humped and two humped Camels or Dromedaries. It looks like a galloping Camel in carvings that are

67. Ixworth Thorpe. Suff.
A libidinous Camel?

obviously copied straight from a Bestiary. It carries no moral meaning and I do not know why we find them in churches unless they carry some of the meanings attached to the Camel.

68. Stowlangtoft. Suff.
A wanton female Camel?

69. Faversham. Kent.
Surprisingly this is a Camel;
kneeling for us.

70. Eynesbury. Beds.
The humble Camel.

71. Denston. Suff.
Possibly a Dromedary.

CAT and see Mouse

Cats are fairly easy to distinguish in carvings.

Pope Gregory IX, 1233, said that heretics worshipped the Devil as a Cat. He was probably giving prominence to an already widely held view. The Waldensians, Cathars and even the Knights Templar were accused of abominable fornication with, or in the presence of Cats. These societies were early Protestant branches of the Church and brutally suppressed, but this only served to reinforce the association of the Cat with Heresy.

Cats have been the familiars of witches for centuries, but I have not found a carving of a cat with a witch figure. Cats see in the dark and thus know 'the orders of Darkness.' So, besides being the sexual associate of witches, they had direct knowledge of Evil. The two traits make the Cat an excellent example of the Devil in animal form. A cat jumping on a mouse as on some fonts (Hodnet) is therefore the

72. Earl Soham. Suff.
A proud heretical Cat.

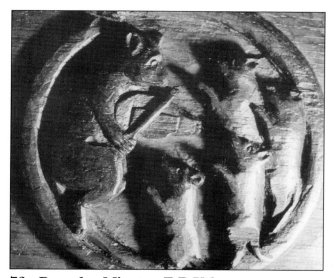

73. Beverley Minster. E.R.Yrks.
The Devil encourages his own.

Devil taking the unwary soul.

At Malvern this story may be more local in its application and includes the idea of role reversal. In this carving mice are hanging a cat. The people of the Middle Ages loved to imagine situations where the humble became mighty and the mighty became weak. This picture (Fig.75) may refer to a story in Piers Plowman(1362) in which the sorely oppressed people of Malvern (Mice) meet on Malvern hill to decide to try to do something about their oppressor, Richard III (Cat). They wish to 'bell the Cat', that is, to make his misdeeds obvious. However none are brave enough and succeed, so the story goes, in turning the tables upon him.

There are numerous pictures of Cats playing fiddles, usually to their kittens, though sometimes alone or to mice. (It has an echo for us in the nursery rhyme; Hey diddle diddle, the Cat and the fiddle.) The Bestiary tells us that mice represent greedy men who seek earthly goods and make the goods of others their prey. The Cat playing the fiddle to them is the Devil urging them on to further rapacious acts.

So when we see Cats or Cat like carvings we must put aside all our present day notions of a cuddly fireside creature. Instead they remind us of the danger of heresy and the sin of desire for riches for their own sake.

In Romanesque carving in England and especially in France we often find feline faces in places that to us appear incongruous. We tend to interpret such

74. Hodnet. Shrops. Font.
The Devil catches the unwary soul.

faces as evil but this may not always be correct. Many such faces or masks as they are properly called, may be an invocation of an idea. They were used to illustrate the four elements, earth, air, fire and water.[4] They may illustrate 'spirit' for instance at Saintes. Here three layers of the arch over the west door show the Lamb of God (God the Son) and the Hand of God (God the Father) separated by a Cat or Lion masque extruding ribbons of foliage. It is tempting to see these as an analogy for the Trinity with the 'Cat' representing the Holy Spirit. (See also the chapter on the Green Man).

75. Gt. Malvern. H&W.
Mice hang the Cat (Richard III)

[4]. See Ref 10 for a fuller discussion under Masque.

76. Saintes. Charente Maritime. Fr.
A feline Masque standing in for the Holy Spirit? with analogies to the Green Man.

77. Fawsley. N'hants.
Greed, mayhem and foul speech aided and abetted by a fiendish Cat family.

78. Hereford Cathedral.
Devil inspired musicians. A Cat and a virile Goat.

79. Northleach. Gloucs.
A reminder to the Cotsworld 'wool barons' not to be too greedy.

CATERPILLAR

The only caterpillar carvings I know in England are on a roof boss in Exeter Cathedral. There they seem to be an expression of all that is beautiful in nature. We find though that the other animals in the same series of roof bosses have a spiritual story to tell so it might be reasonable to assume that so do the Caterpillars.

One story may be that Caterpillars were known as 'Palmer' worms in Medieval times. Palmers were professional pilgrims, and the name had become synonymous with swindler. This might be the coded meaning of this carving. Another idea is that they may also remind us of their destructive habits in the kitchen garden when the lesson would be to beware those who destroy the fruits of other men's labours. However I have not found a Bestiary or Biblical authority for either interpretation. A third and more

80. Exeter Cathedral.
Ambulatory roof boss. Caterpillars feed on flowers. Swindlers? or the earthly phase of an eternal life?

likely idea is that they represent ourselves feeding on spiritual food (tiny roses in this case); the next stages being death (the chrysalis) and resurrection (a butterfly). I have no documentary proof of this but in later, 16th Cent. carvings on bench ends we occasionally find a butterfly. By that time the trio of caterpillar, chrysalis and butterfly portray life, death and resurrection.

81. Othery. Som.
Butterflies

CHARADRIUS OR CALADRIUS

A bird attending to someone lying down is probably a Caladrius.

This is a rather charming mythical white bird that medieval people thought lived in the courts of kings. It had the capacity, when someone was ill, to tell if they would live or die. If they were to die, the bird turned away its head. If they were to live, it would look at the patient, absorb the venom, and fly up towards the sun where the sickness would burn away. The spiritual point is that 'the Caladrius is Christ our Redeemer, wholly white, without sin.' 1.Pet 2:22. 'Who did no sin, neither was guile found in his mouth.' The Bestiary continues, 'our Lord turned his

82. Alne. N.Yrks.
A Caladrius (Christ) takes the illness from a sick king (sinful man) who will now survive.

face from the Jews because of their unbelief and turned instead to the heathen,' and points to Is.53:4. 'For he hath borne our griefs and carried our sorrows.'

We can see a Caladrius at Alne. One may be carved on a misericord at Carlisle. Here it looks just like a double headed eagle, 'ducally gorged' which means it could be of heraldic significance for a local family. Or it could just possibly be a Caladrius where the carver has tried to show the bird's two different actions in the one carving.

83. Carlisle. Cumb.
A 'ducally gorged' double headed bird that may tell the Caladrius' story.

CENTAUR

The Centaur is half man and half horse. It is difficult to understand, because the same figure may express two contrasting themes.

A Centaur shooting an arrow is often called Sagittarius because it would have been well known in that form as a sign of the Zodiac. The meaning of the Centaur/Sagittarius in the church context is more complicated. The human half is Christ. One Bestiary writer compares the bow to the cross, and the arrow to the Holy Spirit that metaphorically left the earthly body of Christ in order to save those he loved, and those who were in Hell and wanted help from Him. This is a direct reference to the Harrowing of Hell. (see p139). The nether half, says the writer, signifies His vengeance upon the Jews.

At Exeter and Kencot we see Christ depicted this way conquering Satan. On the font at Hook Norton the Centaur / Sagittarius faces a water carrier, Aquarius. This image may refer to Christ and the waters of baptism. The church leaflet also suggests that the Centaur is shooting the one who brings the Flood, metaphorically in this case Aquarius; and that this act contrasts with regeneration in the waters of baptism in the font.

A Centaur shoots an arrow towards a double headed eagle at Elkstone, Glos. The

84. Kencot. Oxon.
Tympanum. Christ as the Centaur/Sagittarius kills Satan as Leviathan.

arrow misses intentionally. Both the arrow from the Centaur, Christ, and the double headed eagle are symbols of the Holy Spirit. There is a connection even if it is obscure.

The Centaur with a cross in one hand and foliage in the other at Ault Hucknall is probably also Christ. The explanation lies in the concept that Christ conducts us across the threshold of death much as Chiron conducts people across the Styx. Chiron is shown in an old Herbal holding Artemesia, a healing herb.[5] So this particular carving may show Christ with the herb of healing and the cross of salvation ready to conduct us to a new life.

Centaurs are also animals with a reputation for large sexual appetites and in that form they are symbols of lust and adultery.

[5]. Ref 52. p364

47

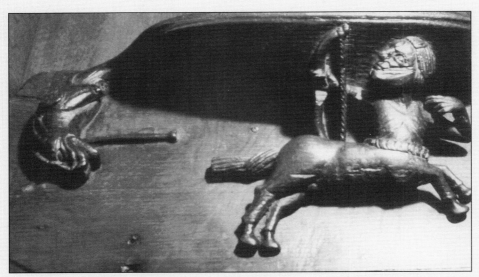

85. Exeter Cathedral.
Christ as Centaur uses the Holy Spirit to slay evil.

86. Elkstone. Gloucs.
A Centaur Christ and two symbols for the Holy Spirit; an arrow and a double headed Eagle.

87. Hook Norton. Oxon . Font.
A Sagittarius Centaur and Aquarius the water carrier.

88. Ault Hucknall. Derbys.
Christ as Centaur/Chiron who can lead us over the river of death.

89. Exeter Cathedral.
A roof boss; possibly an evil Centaur.

COCK

The Cock is very easy to recognise and it has many associations and meanings. It appears with St Peter in the story of the Crucifixion. Jn13:38 'The Cock shall not crow till thou hast denied me thrice.' So we often find it as one of the many symbols of the Passion.

An early Pope once decreed that all churches should display an image of the Cock where it can tell the hour of service in honour of St. Peter. This is the reason for the very common Cock as a weathervane. In this position it also has another function. The Basilisk fears only the Cock and the Weasel. So our weathervane can also act as an effective deterrent to the lethal glance of the Basilisk and therefore a useful weapon in the fight against evil.

There is a little moral story in the charming farmyard scene of a Cock and a Hen at Tewkesbury. The Cock when he finds some food, calls his mate to share it; and is therefore a symbol of Liberality.

The Cock heralds the Day after the night of Darkness. As Bede says 'the Cock is like the souls of the Just, waiting for dawn after the darkness of the world's light' and so may be a symbol for the Resurrection and for Vigilance. The Bestiary says that its song brings hope to everyone, eases the pain of the sick, cools the fevered brow, and brings back Faith where that has lapsed.

There are pictures of Cocks fighting. Medieval preachers say that this is a picture of Christians striving for Christ.

Finally the Reynard stories, Chaucer's Tale of the Nun's Priest, and no doubt others, all tell of various escapades involving Chanticleer the Cock, and his wife Pertelot. Chanticleer is the guard, if he fails, the fox will kill the flock. (see Fig.181) We see the fox, the Cock and other farmyard animals fleeing from an infuriated housewife.

In summary and in relation to the majority of the Cocks that we see, 'Watch and pray lest ye enter into temptation.' Mk 14:38.

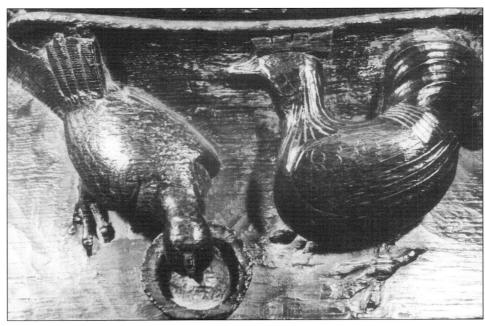

90. Tewkesbury. Gloucs.
The Cock exhibits 'Liberality' as he shares his good fortune with his good lady.

91. St Mawgan in Pydar. Corn.
A Cock for St Peter.

92. Hatch Beauchamp. Som.
'Christians striving for Christ.'

93. Wells Cathedral.
A Cock crowing to announce the 'New Day' or Chanticleer warning his flock.

CRAB AND SCORPION

The Crab usually has many legs, but when there are only four or six it can be very difficult to distinguish it from the Scorpion although the Scorpion should have a prominent tail. Both feature in the Bestiary and both are signs of the Zodiac.

We are most likely to notice the Crab as Cancer the Zodiacal sign for the height of summer, 22 June to 22 July. It appears at the top centre of the band of carving on the arches of some Norman churches. The outer layer of the arch often represents the Zodiac that lay in the outermost of the heavenly spheres and therefore nearest to God. The Zodiac marks the path of the sun through the heavens and the Zodiac formed the eighth heaven in the Ptolemaic system. It is very much an ultimate boundary between our universe and God. Single Zodiac signs on an archway may be a shorthand way of saying that this layer represents the Zodiac, earth and all the other heavens are below it.

The Sun is often a metaphor for Christ. So too may be the Crab in the context of the Zodiac. The story is that just as the Crab cannot go straight by land or sea; just so the Sun cannot go higher in this part of the Zodiac (June). The Bestiary writers are forcing the simile at this point. The Crab near the top of the arch equals the sun that equals Christ so the carver has an appropriate animal metaphor to place near the keystone position. (Fig.94)

The writers use another analogy to compare Christ to the Crab. They say that Christ, in his humanity on earth, went from side to side because he feared the pagans and the Jews.

The Bestiary writer tells us that the Crab longs for oyster flesh. It waits till the shells are slightly open then pushes a pebble gently inside to stop them closing. The moral point is that crabs are like people who practise unnatural tricks and use cunning to further their desires. They feed on the distress of others. Therefore, they tell us: 'Be content with what is yours. Do not try to gain advantage by injuring others.'

So Cancer, the Crab, may have one or two meanings or even both at once, according to how we read the context.

94. Aulnay. Charente Maritime. Fr.
A Crab above the head of Christ, top centre of an entry portal.

95. Birkin. N.Yrks.
A Crab at the top of the arch over the S. door.

96. Letton. H&W.
A Frog with a Crab or Scorpion.

SCORPION

The Scorpion too they said could represent God, for it is a bold and pugnacious beast. God was a Scorpion when he reprehended the Jews.[6] The Bestiary gives it a sting in the tail with which it pierces the palm of the hand. In this mode it signifies the Devil and those who serve him.

As a sign of the Zodiac it belongs to late October and most of November.

[6]. Ref 63.

97. Chartres. Eure et Loir.
A fine Scorpion.

98. Birkin. N.Yrks.
A Scorpion on the arch over the S. door.

CRANE and also see Heron and Stork

There are three sorts of long legged birds that we might encounter in carvings, the Crane, the Stork and the Heron. They are difficult to distinguish. The Crane should carry a stone in one claw. The others are just long legged birds with long beaks.

One might well ask what are Cranes doing in English carvings? They are not native birds. The Bestiary writers illustrate their significance with this story. At night one

99. Denston. Suff.
A sentinel Crane with his stone.

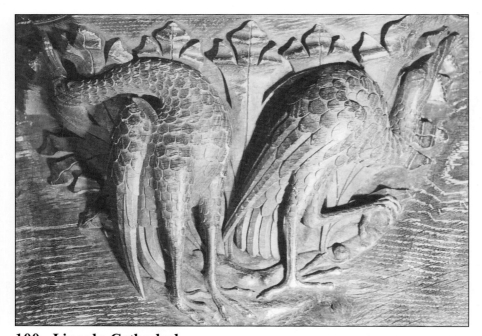

100. Lincoln Cathedral.
A pair of Cranes; sharing responsibilities within the monastic community.

of a group of Cranes is on sentinel duty around their leader, a task he undertakes willingly because he knows that he will be sharing his responsibilities. The members of a monastic order do likewise. In order to stay awake he holds a stone in one claw. Should he fall asleep the stone will fall, so waking him. The moral is that in just such a way must we all be vigilant against sin.

We see it very often in churches in the context of Aesop's fable about the Fox and the Crane or Stork. In this fable the fox invites the bird to dinner but serves the meal on a plate; so the poor Crane or Stork is unable to partake because of his long bill. In return the Crane or Stork invites the fox to a dinner that he serves in a long narrow necked jar, so only the bird can partake. The fox cannot complain for the Crane or Stork has repaid him in his own coin. 'Do as you would be done by', as the Victorians might say. This is not a particularly Christian message, rather the opposite; but it is an improving tale and in that sense the Church has seized on it to make a general moral point.

Cranes also have an annual battle with pygmies according to very early writers, but we do not know why. The 'boy' riding a

101. Chester Cathedral.
Aesop's fable of the Fox and the Crane.

Crane at Lincoln is probably just such a pygmy.

So Cranes are there both to encourage Christian watchfulness, and/or as in the Aesop fable to promote fairness and equality in all our social relationships.

102. Lincoln Cathedral.
A Pygmy fighting with three Cranes.

Illust. 1
The Sentinel Crane

CROCODILE and see Hydrus

The Bestiary Crocodile and therefore the illustrations from which the carver had to work bear absolutely no relation to our idea of a Crocodile.

The Bestiary writers describe it with terrible claws and a mouth that opens by moving the upper jaw upwards. To illustrate this last point the early illustrators show an animal with the head reversed. See the animal at Lower Swell. It is much more often shown swallowing the Hydrus and in this guise it achieves a wide variety of forms. (See them in the chapter about the Hydrus.)

It is the forerunner of the Dragon slain by St. George. It is also the original for Job's Leviathan whose jaws become the gaping Jaws of Hell.

103. Kilpeck. H&W.
Crocodile swallowing the Hydrus.

It lives on land and water and therefore it lives a double life. This makes it an example of the Arch Deceiver and as the jaws of hell it is Satan at his most terrifying.

It sheds tears after eating a whole person; the original for our phrase 'Crocodile's tears.'

The Crocodile is Satan and Satan will ultimately be destroyed.

104. Lower Swell. Gloucs.
The upside down head on a Crocodile

105. Topsham. Devon. Font.
Crocodile swallowing the Hydrus.

106. Burton Dassett. Warw.
Crocodile with Hydrus.

DEVIL and also see Tutivillus

The Devil needs no introduction and I am including him because he has so many animal disguises. We can think of him in two ways. Medieval people thought of him as having a body, a mind, and spirit, and believed that he lay in wait manipulating the powers of this world to his own ends. Modern man favours the idea that he is inside us, an evil 'Hyde' at war with the good 'Jekyll' that we all hope to be. Either way his features are the most horrible and terrifying that the artist and carver can produce.

107. Beverley Minster. N. Parclose screen.
The Devil lies in wait.

108. Charlton Mackrell. Som.
Tutivillus with a list of sins and a bag in which to store it.

He has several minions. A special one is Tutivillus, the Titivally of Shakespeare, (see p.253 & Fig.108) who collected the sins of speech. He listened in church for idle chatter, especially that between women. He checked on the cleric making sure that he did not mumble his prayers. He wrote all the wrong doings down on a long scroll that he placed in a sack and kept till the dreadful Day of Judgement.

The Devil has many animal disguises; such as the Amphisbaena, and Ape, the Cat and the Crocodile; and he was always known as the Arch Deceiver. The medieval preacher needed examples from life or larger than life situations to bring home to his flock the devious ways of Satan. Many of the animals in this book demonstrate the sinful traits that Christianity has always sought to eliminate.

Some examples of the devil gathering wrong doers include the Devil carrying off a man with too short a spoon. 'For he who sups with the Devil needs a long spoon.' We can interpret the story of Jack the Giant killer in several ways from the Freudian to the Christian. The latter includes the conquest of evil by the faith of the Christian. Fig.113.

A Dragon on its back in the stocks depicts an ultimate degradation for Satan.

109. New Coll. Oxf.
The Devil carries off someone who used too short a spoon.

110. Horning. Norf.
A Devil prods a soul into the flaming Hell mouth of Leviathan. A defeated Devil in the stocks above.

111. Freckenham. Suff.
A Devil prods a sinner into Hell's mouth.

112. Hemingbrough. N.Yrks.
The Devil in person playing his musical instrument.

113. New Coll. Oxf.
Jack and the bean(pea) stalk. The evil giant eats lambs(Christians) for his supper.

114. Faversham. Kent.
The Devil carries off some sinner.

DOG

It is not difficult to recognise Dogs although it is easy to confuse some of them with Beavers whose story includes attention to the nether regions.

In the time since the domestication of the first Dogs there have grown up many strange and sometimes powerful symbolic associations. Only a few persist in sculpture. One is of the Dog as a symbol of undying love and faithfulness, Fido, which means the faithful one. This seems to be one of the commonest meanings when he is alone or accompanying a woman. Tombs often carry

115. Lakenheath. Suff.
A Dog heals by licking.

the effigies of a knight and his lady. His feet will be resting on a Lion, while hers will be on a Dog.

Dogs can heal wounds by licking them said the Bestiary writers. Some carvings emphasise this point with a very large tongue soothing an open sore on a rump.

In the same way the writers say we as sinners can heal our wounds when we lay them bare in confession.

St Roche, who usually has terrible sores on his legs, is accompanied by a dog. He had helped many

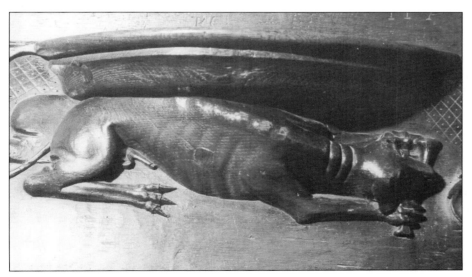

116. Christchurch. Dorset.
'Envy gnaws at the soul like a dog gnaws at a bone.'

people stricken by the plague until he caught it himself. He went into the woods where he was cared for by a dog and miraculously fed. He recovered and then continued to help other plague victims. He was the saint to invoke for help against the pestilence

The Bible in Prov.26:11 says, 'as a dog returns to his vomit, so a fool returneth to his folly.' A point reaffirmed by the Bestiary that says that the Dog can represent those who fall into sin again after they have confessed.

There are other meanings. A Dog gnawing a bone tells us of envy. For 'envy gnaws at the soul as a dog gnaws at a bone.'[7] Backbiters too gnaw their hands as dogs gnaw at bones. Preachers used the example of the common situation in which a dog behind a fence barks at passers-by to illustrate the same point. The fact that he is shut in makes him envious of the freedom of those outside.

117. Monksilver. Som.
The hunt. Good pursues evil.

We find other less pleasant associations in the apparent sexiness of dogs. 'Prostitutes serve in all lechery as hounds do.' (Bartholomeus Anglicus) Fig.377. p.188.

The Chase, whether of stag or fox or hare, was a major feature of life for those with land or the rights to the land. That it appears in carvings is no surprise, for the local Abbot was often no mean hunter. In a church context the Dog taking part in a hunt carries a meaning beyond the mere illustration of this everyday activity. The Dog in pursuit of hares and foxes, both animals with generally evil associations, is Good in pursuit of Evil. In this connection it is worth mentioning that the Dominicans were known as the Domini Canes, the Hounds of

118. Gt. Malvern.
A relaxed but hungry dog.

God. (A rather nice pun on their name.)

If the hunted is a stag and surrounded by hounds, the picture carries the opposite meaning. The stag is Christ. The hounds are the forces of evil.

The Bestiary also has the little tale of a dog carrying a piece of meat and crossing a river. In the water it sees a reflection and opens its mouth to grab the other piece of non-existent meat and in so doing loses the reality in exchange for a shadow. I have yet to recognise this story in carving.

119. Wells Cathedral.
A faithful Dog.

Some dogs, unlike most of the carved animals, are probably just illustrations of ordinary domestic scenes. The Talbot Dog was a long eared hunting dog famous for a keen sense of smell. (For the Dog and hare at Kilpeck see note 11.) Others scratch an ear in luxurious idleness or snooze on feather cushions.

All these different ideas mean that there are several possibilities to consider when we find a carving of a dog.

[7]. Ref 49.

120. Les Andelys. Eure. Fr.
A Dog to compare with the Beaver Fig. 50. p. 32.

121. Astley. Warw.
A Talbot hunting dog.

DOLPHIN

The carvers usually show Dolphins as fairly large single fish, with the characteristic arched form we recognise when we see dolphins surfacing as they travel through the water. We of course know that it is really a mammal rather than a fish, but that is not relevant to the story. There are some other marine creatures that may cause confusion; these include the Aspidochelone, the Serra, Leviathan and an ordinary Fish.

The Dolphin is a large and independent animal. There were many stories of Dolphins who had saved shipwrecked sailors, (but only the sailors who had not eaten Dolphin flesh). This concept carries over into Christian symbolism making the Dolphin a picture of Salvation.

The story of Jonah and the whale becomes partially amalgamated with the Dolphin story because the way the 'Whale' saves Jonah is analogous way to the way Dolphins save sailors. Other candidates for the real whale in that story include the Aspidochelone and Leviathan. However the spiritual parable is similar whichever large sea creature we choose for Jonah's whale. The Jonah story is a 'Type' or metaphor for the Descent into Hell and subsequent Resurrection.

So the Dolphin can mean more than Salvation, and include the ideas of deliverance from Death, and of the Resurrection.

122. Ashwell. Herts.
A Dolphin to remind us of Salvation.

123. Swavesey. Camb.
A Dolphin for Deliverance.

65

DOVES

The species of a given single bird without obvious characteristics can be almost impossible to identify in carving. It is only by their actions for instance that we can be certain that any particular carving represents a Dove.

The Dove descending is a universal figure for the Holy Spirit. A Dove with a branch is the Dove that Noah sent forth. It returned at first with nothing, but later with an olive branch thereby telling Noah that all would soon be well. We can understand it as a symbolic peace offering following the apparent destruction of the world. Similarly for the Christian, outside the Church all is desolation, only inside is there safety and God's forgiveness.

We find Doves feeding from a cup and Doves feeding on grapes in a thousand places across the land. They are Christian souls benefiting from the redeeming blood of Christ.

124. Bishopsteignton. Devon.
A Dove feeds on grapes, the 'blood' of Christ.

125. Hampnett. Gloucs.
Doves (Christians) drinking from the communion cup.

Turtle Doves mated for life, and are therefore an example to humankind. By extension, the writers hope that widows will not look elsewhere when their husbands die.

Preachers are like Doves for they choose the best scriptures as the Dove chooses the best grain. Doves nest in holes in rocks as preachers take refuge in their belief in Christ.

Doves fly in flocks as preachers gather in flocks and follow good works. 'For such good works as we do are steps towards God'.

Finally the Bible admonishes us to be as harmless as Doves. Matt.10:16

126. Cartmel. Cumb.
Possibly two Doves choosing the best scriptures.

127. Hilfield. Dorset.
The Dove of the Holy Spirit.

128. Spaxton. Som.
A Dove with an olive branch, to tell us that all will be well in a renewed world.

67

DRAGONS

Proper Dragons have four feet; the twin footed varieties are Wyverns and both have the same significance. In practice many winged lizards or snake like creatures sometimes with more than one head, serve for the artist's idea of a Dragon.

The Bestiary states that 'the Dragon is the greatest of all Serpents.' Western civilisation seems to have always understood

129. Beverley Min. E.R.Yorks.
A Dragon seeking whom he may devour.

that the Dragon is wild, fierce and evil whereas for instance Chinese dragons are good. The Church uses this beast to give concrete form to the most destructive aspects of Evil.

The Dragon in Rev 12:3. had seven heads and ten horns and a tail that swept a third of the stars from heaven. His defeat in Rev 12:7-9 represents the end of the heavenly struggle between good and evil.

There are three famous stories about **St. Michael.**

He is first of the seven archangels and the leader of the heavenly host that kills Satan in Dragon form in Rev 12;7-9. We often

130. Lew Trenchard. Devon.
St Michael weighs souls.

68

see him thrusting a spear into a fire breathing Dragon that lies beneath him. An action that has close parallels to Christ's when Harrowing Hell.

He also weighs souls, much as souls were weighed before Osiris in ancient Egypt. The picture usually includes Satan trying to influence the result by pulling on the side of the soul's misdeeds.

St George.

St George slays the Dragon that demanded the daily sacrifice of a maiden from the

131. Hemingbrough. N.Yorks.
St George slays the Dragon.

townspeople of Silene. The story originated in Egypt where they ritually slew Seth-Typhon on April 23rd, St George's day. He was the producer of drought, sterility and famine.

St Margaret

She is famous because she escapes after being swallowed by a Dragon. In her story the local governor, a particularly nasty suitor, woes her by force. She refuses his advances so he throws her into a dungeon where she meets a Dragon. It swallows her. She makes the sign of the cross. Immediately the Dragon splits open and she escapes. She has become the patron saint of midwives and is the third person one might find in combat with a Dragon.

There are a few carvings of someone giving a cake or a bun to a Dragon. This almost certainly refers to the story of Bel and the Dragon found in the Apocryphal last chapter of Daniel. Daniel shows the King that the priests are deceiving him over his favourite god, Bel. Daniel goes further and offers to slay the Dragon that inhabits the same place as this God. This

132. Sherborne. Dorset.
St Margaret rises out of the Dragon by the power of the Cross.

69

he promises to do without sword or staff. He makes a noxious cake containing pitch that he puts in the Dragon's mouth; 'and so the Dragon burst in sunder.' Dan.Apoc.v.27.

I think this is the meaning of the bench end carvings at Tuttinton and Horning and also possibly of the Tympanum at Down St. Mary. (Note 2) The Tuttington animal is properly a griffin.

133. Isle Abbotts. Som. Font.
The Devil 'down and out', renounced and slain by baptism.

This is another Old Testament picture, or 'Type', of Christ in Hell and of his victory there over Satan.

On a font at Isle Abbotts they carved the dragon upside down to show his 'defeated status. Another defeated Dragon is in the stocks at Horning. Others swallow Judas or other nameless sinners; all lie in wait for good and bad alike.

134. Crowcombe. Som.
Naked but unafraid against the twin headed monster. See p.210.

135. Horning. Norf.
The Devil on his back, held in the stocks.

136. Down St Mary. Devon.
Tympanum. Probably Daniel with a quietened Lion and defeated Dragon.

137. Horning. Norf.
Probably Daniel placing a cake of pitch in the mouth of Bel the Dragon.

138. Tuttinton. Norf.
Possibly an allusion to Daniel's defeat of Bel the Dragon.

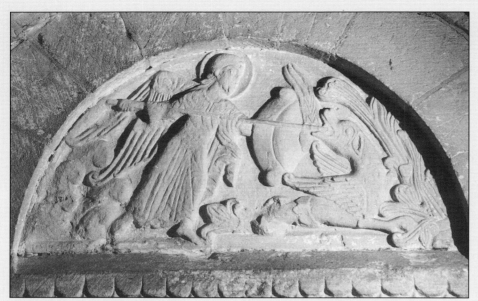

139. Moreton Valance. Gloucs.
Tympanum. St Michael v. The Satanic Dragon.

140. Withersfield Suff.
St Michael weighing souls.

141. Deerhurst. Gloucs.
One of many similar Dragons in early churches either guarding archways or maybe posing a threat to the faithful.

BIGORNE

The Dragon usually credited with swallowing Judas might be the Bigorne instead. This is a mythical beast and not mentioned in the Bestiary. M.D.Anderson suggests that the following may be the story for this carving, because there is a very similar picture, but depicting the Bigorne, in a mural at the châteaux of Villeneuve-Lembron, (Puy-de-Dôme). Obedient husbands on which the Bigorne fed were in abundant supply, so it grew fat. This was in contrast to Chicheface, (Fr.Chichevache; Thin cow) which fed on obedient wives. The male of medieval times considered obedient wives to be in very short supply, so Chiceface nearly starved. (Fig. 143, 144).

142. Worcester Cathedral.
The Bigorne swallows yet another obedient husband. Also known as Judas in the jaws of Satan.

143. Villeneuve Lembron. Château. Puy de Dôme.
The Bigorne makes a meal of an obedient husband.

144. Villeneuve Lembron. Château. Puy de Dôme.
Chicheface, thin cow, finds an all too scarce obedient wife.

74

EAGLE

The most common place to see an eagle in a church is as an Eagle lectern; but why did they choose an Eagle? Is it that it is the noblest of birds as the lion is the noblest of beasts? Is it just the best shape to be bearing an open book? It is more than these.

The story starts in the Bestiary. The Eagle alone could fly undazzled towards the sun. Sometimes non Eagle chicks would get into his nest. To test these and his own offspring the Eagle took them all up with him. Those that turned away from the sun he throws out as being unworthy. Thus metaphorically it is only the Eagle that can take us into the presence of God who we

146. Wolborough. Devon.
An Eagle lectern.

145. Forrabury. Corn.
An eagle plunges into water for rejuvenation.
c.f. Illust. 2 p.78.

learn about from the Book. The book is the Bible for, 'In the beginning was the Word, and the Word was with God, and the Word was God.' Jn.1:1. Therefore we not only have Eagle lecterns but also an Eagle as the emblem of St John whose gospel begins in that dramatic way.

(The Greek word 'Logos' which is here translated by 'The Word', carries a much wider meaning than merely a written or spoken word. There were many strands of thought from Greek philosophy including the idea of 'a divine reason' that permeates all things and of a timeless something that was always there before all things. Our concept 'Word' hardly does justice to it but that is the phrase we have and the one that Christians down the ages acknowledge. The three definitions in that first verse of Jn1 go some way to covering the idea that he was trying to convey.)

We also find that the Eagle is one of the four beasts of both Rev 4.6-8. and of Ezekiel's vision, 1:5-14 & 10:14. (See Tetramorph). An Eagle bearing a scroll in his beak is an emblem of St John and we often find it in company with the other three evangelical symbols.

When the Eagle grows old it flies even higher. As it approaches nearer the sun, the feathers scorch and the heat burns off the membrane of the eye. It then plunges into a fountain that restores strength to wings and clarity to eyes. This makes a parallel to

147. Castle Frome. H&W.
An eagle as one of the four evangelistic symbols.

148. Brent Knoll. Som.
An Eagle plus scroll for St John.

Baptism that for an adult represents a totally new beginning to the spiritual life. We may find Eagles on fonts both for this reason and because it was an early symbol of the Holy Spirit in its double headed form. This latter idea was carried over from the Roman way of showing power and victory. Like some other Roman symbols it appears in early Christian pictures, then as an example of omnipotence, slightly later as a picture of the Holy Spirit.

Elisha received a double portion of the Spirit and some double headed Eagle carvings may illustrate this episode. II Kings 2:9

The Bestiary also tells us that the Eagle can see fish as they swim below and will dive to capture them. 'So Christ came down to earth to capture the souls of men out of the sea of this troubled world.' This may be the meaning of the Ribbesford carving.

The artists of the Middle Ages sometimes use the Eagle as a symbol of the Ascension.

Occasionally preachers used it in a negative sense, confusing it with the vulture, saying that it fed on stinking carrion and could thus be a figure of evil Pride. I do not know of an example in carving.

149. Hodnet. Shrops. Font.
The start of a new spiritual life with the help of the Holy Spirit.

150. Earl Soham. Suff.
A double headed Eagle or a Caladrius?

151. Ribbesford. H&W.
An Eagle takes up its young and catches fish.

77

152. Minstead. Hants. Font.

A double headed eagle, a dove? and a tree of Life? Two symbols of the Holy Spirit.

Illust. 2.
Three facets of the Eagle's story.

153. Stogursey. Som.
A double headed Eagle, the power of the Spirit.

78

ELEPHANT

The illustrators of the Bestiary had considerable difficulty with the Elephant so some of the carvings based on their pictures do need a sympathetic imagination to recognise them.

'There is no beast greater than this', says the Bestiary. No wonder that the Elephant was an object of fascination and great awe. Few of the ordinary people had seen a real elephant, although one was given to Henry III in 1255

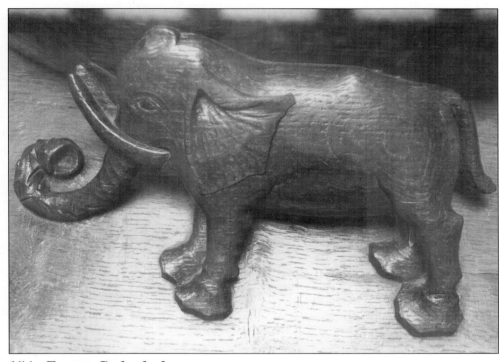

154. Exeter Cathedral.
Probably the best and one of the earliest Elephant carvings.

and survived for several years in the Tower. Sketches of it may form the basis for the carving on an Exeter misericord that is the most lifelike of the medieval ones in England. Most Elephants in carvings have a castle on their backs. The Bestiaries point out that Indians and Persian fought each other from these towers and they soon became an integral part of the Elephant picture. In practice every animal with a tower is an Elephant and virtually every Elephant has such a tower. There were several well-known stories about the Elephant and each one gives us a different symbolic meaning that I have highlighted for the sake of clarity.

Firstly, they lived for three hundred years but only had intercourse once, and that only after she had given him the fruit of the mandrake, a famous aphrodisiac. The writers make a direct parallel with Adam and Eve, for Adam did not 'know' Eve while they were in Paradise. Symbol 1. **Chastity.** The relative sexlessness of the Elephant being used later as an exemplar of the Virgin Mary.

The Bestiary states that their knees and therefore their legs cannot bend so they must sleep by leaning against trees. The cunning hunter cuts half through a likely tree that collapses when the Elephant goes to sleep. He is unable to rise. The other twelve Elephants in the herd (the Prophets) surround him but find they cannot help. A great Elephant (the Law) also cannot help. A tiny Elephant (Jesus Christ) 'who was the greatest of all in that he humbled himself before death', lifts the fallen Elephant easily. So the second symbol is **Salvation.**

Third: The Elephant gives birth in water to protect the baby from the Dragon, its most fierce enemy. So there is an association with **Baptism** as on a font at Dunkeswell. The Christian, like the Elephant, starts his new life through the medium of water.

Fourth: In a fight with the Dragon, shown as a python like creature in a Bestiary, both die. The Dragon strangles the Elephant. The Elephant falls and in his fall he crushes the Dragon to death. 'So the Devil suffocates in coils of sin those who would make their way towards heaven.' There is such a picture in a 12th

155. Carlisle. Cumb.
The Serpent coils round the Elephant.

Cent. Bestiary.[8] The picture is so very close to the carving at Carlisle that it could well have been the source for the carver. It is certainly the most unrealistic of all Elephant pictures. Illust. 3.

The many Elephant and Castle carvings probably also represent the **Indestructible Church** supported on a firm foundation of Faith and the Virgin Mary. A good preacher could easily expand on both these themes.

The Bestiary, and therefore carvings of single Elephants, encourage us to remember several things. These include; the trampling down of sin; the power of Jesus Christ to raise one up for Salvation, and that it is possible to live a long life in continence.

Illust. 3.
A Bestiary Elephant and a entwining Dragon/Serpent.

[8] . Ref 58.

80

156. Cartmel Priory. Cumb.
An elephant leans against a tree.

157. Dunkeswell. Devon. Font.
An Elephant gives birth or defeats the serpent in the water.

158. Denston. Suff.
An Elephant for chastity and/or the indestructible Church.

FABLES

Every generation needs to be able to present home truths in a palatable fashion and never more so than when helping children to explore the realities of the big, wide world. This starts with nursery rhymes and when a little older there are cycles of stories such as those about Brer Rabbit. The Middle Ages has a multitude of stories about Reynard the Fox, Noble the Lion, Isengrin the Wolf and the rest that fulfil the same function. One can identify with Reynard as one can with Brer Rabbit. Predating even

159. Gloucester Cathedral.
Ass and lapdog.

the Reynard stories are Aesop's fables expressing wisdom and advice in proverbial mode.

There are carvings of several at Gloucester; including **the Ass and the Lapdog** (see under Ass); and **the Fox and the sick Lion**. In this fable the sick lion approaches the fox's den and notes many tracks leading to the den but none leaving it. 'He is wise who is warned by the misfortunes of others.'

There are many pictures of the **Fox and the Crane or Stork**. See under Crane for the story.

The **Fox and the Grapes** is another sporadic carving. The Fox desires

160. Gloucester Cathedral.
A sick Lion and a Fox with a urinal. The latter to show his false pretences.

some grapes that are just out of reach. He tries everything but cannot obtain them and turns away saying that they would be sour anyway. The source for our phrase 'sour grapes.' Fig.163.

There is a part of the Lohengrin story shown at Exeter; the **'Chevalier au Cygne'**. Lohengrin, son of Percival, arrives at Antwerp in a skiff drawn by a swan. He champions Elsa and becomes her husband on the condition that she does not ask him of his origins. She does so; therefore he disappears. The moral is, 'That one should keep one's promise however much the circumstances would seem to exonerate one from doing so'.' Unfortunately we cannot say for certain that the carver intends this meaning.

161. Holt. H&W.
The Fox and the Stork.

Sir Yvain

The rather curious picture of a Castle where a Portcullis descends on the hindquarters of a Horse refers to a popular episode in the Arthurian legends. In outline the story is this. Sir Yvain mortally wounds a knightly enemy and follows him back to his castle. The wounded knight reaches safety through the inner portcullis but dies soon afterwards. The portcullises fall. The outer one cuts Sir Yvain's horse in half. He is now trapped between the inner and outer portcullis. A young lady befriends him and gives him a magic ring that will make him invisible. He uses this to avoid detection in the ensuing hue and cry, but falls in love with the wife of his former enemy. The young lady carries his protestations of love to the new widow. Sir Yvain comes out of hiding and admits the awful thing that he has done. She forgives him for killing her former husband. They marry and live happily ever afterwards.

The spiritual message is this; here is an important example of the admission of Sin and the rewards of Forgiveness; a perfect parallel for the situation of the Christian.[9]

162. Exeter Cathedral.
'Le Chevalier au Cygne'. A story about keeping one's promises.

The Flight of Alexander.

This was a famous tale amongst the Romances of the Middle Ages. Alexander having conquered everywhere of significance on earth now wishes to explore the heavens. He places himself in a basket that he harnesses to a pair of Griffins. These he encourages to fly ever higher and farther by holding some meat on the points of a pair of spears such that the meat is always just out of their reach. They stay aloft for ten days until God persuades the Griffins to drop him many miles from his army. Alexander has to admit that he can find no limit to this region of mystery.[10]

This is an example of the Sin of Pride. A man, even so great a one as Alexander, attempts to wrest God's secrets from him by Learning, but all he finds is mystery after mystery. We find an alternative interpretation in 'Cy nous dit'. It says that the episode illustrates man's hunger for the beauty of Heaven

163. Faversham. Kent.
The Fox cannot quite reach the grapes. 'So they must be sour grapes.'

Our ancestors loved riddles. Riddling became a high literary art form in the middle ages and many were capable of producing two answers, one salacious, one more prosaic. There were riddle 'contests' in which the game was to reply to one riddle request with another usually even more exotic and impossible. The story of the **Clever Daughter**, Queen Disa or **Grania**, belongs to this genre.

There is a group of carvings that immediately arouses one's curiosity. They are usually of a woman, naked, covered in a net, and holding a hare or rabbit under the arm. She is riding a goat but has one foot on the ground. She is obviously travelling with a purpose. One may see examples at Gloucester, Worcester, Beverley St. Mary and York Minster. (Fig.165) Curiously at Exeter there is a man instead. The story goes back to pre-Christian times and has evolved in various ways in different cultures. A composite of the main themes goes thus. A peasant girl finds a golden mortar and runs to tell her father. He says, 'We must give it to the King.' She says 'Without the pestle there is no point, for the King will think that we have stolen it.' Which is just what happens. The father ends up in prison; and says 'if only I had listened to my daughter.' The King, who also happens

164. Lincoln Cathedral.
Sir Yvain's horse is trapped by the portcullis. A story about Christ's forgiveness.

to be looking for a suitable wife, hears of this saga and asks this Clever Daughter to come to him. If she solves the following riddle she may be his wife. 'Come to me not clothed and not naked, not riding and not walking, not in the road and not out of the road, and bring a present that is not a present.' This is the picture that we see in the carving. The hare is the gift that is no gift, for it will run away when it is presented. The net is not proper clothing, and there is one foot half touching the ground the far side of the goat. There are many delightful variations, especially in Celtic and Central European folk tales. In the Gesta Romanorum, a sort of source book for mediaeval preachers, we find a similar tale. The King asks the girl to make a shirt from a piece of linen three inches long and broad. She retaliates by asking for a vessel in which to make it. In the normal riddle series various other improbabilities will be produced one after the other. However in the Christian preacher's tale the whole story

165. Worcester Cathedral.
The story of the Clever Daughter; a parable about the Incarnation.

ends here. She makes the shirt. He makes her his wife.

The preacher indicates that God is the King and the girl is the Virgin Mary. Gabriel is the messenger going to and fro. The scrap of linen is the working of the Holy Spirit in her. The vessel to make it in is her womb. She makes a shirt that is; 'The humanity of Christ, which humanity has wrought in her.' The Heavenly Father crowns her Queen of Heaven. So, unlikely as it seems, the Clever Daughter carvings are probably a reminder of the doctrine of the **Incarnation**. The sexual associations of goat, hare and nakedness all take a back seat; we are not here looking at 'exemplars of lust' as is sometimes stated. The roses behind the goat on the Worcester misericord, which are one of the attributes of the Virgin, seem to

166. Beverley St Mary. E.R.Yorks.
The Flight of Alexander.

confirm this interpretation. The hare, which they thought was able to conceive without male intervention, is another attribute of the Virgin. The goat, which on the one hand is sexual, on the other we associate with a result of sexuality, that is fertility. She holds the goat's horn that was the original for the Horn of Plenty.

We find here that all the components of the picture complement different aspects of the story of the Virgin Mary. The connection between the two stories is much clearer where the matter is discussed at length in Ref 41. and see 48 & 53.

Tristan and Iseult. Although there is no animal connection this story features so often in company with the others that an outline may help. The usual carving pictures a man's head peering through some branches, while below a young man and young woman converse.

King Mark is the head in the tree. The lady is his wife and she is having an affair with Tristan. The King plans to catch them together but they see his face reflected in

167. Lincoln Cathedral.
The Legend of Tristan and Iseult. A parable that shows us that God knows our secrets even if the world does not.

some water. They realise what he is doing and modify their conversation accordingly, so that all appears very Platonic. The Moral ... That individuals, knowing that God knows all that we do, should avoid sin and occasions for sin; as the lovers did after seeing King Mark's face reflected in the pool.

[9]. See Ref 9.

[10]. Ref 42.

168. Charney Bassett. Oxon.
Tympanum. The Flight of Alexander. Either a story about pride or about hunger for the beauty of Heaven

FISH

From earliest times the Fish has been a Christian symbol. The first letters of the Greek words for Jesus / Christ / of God / the Son / Saviour make ΙΧΘΥΣ / ICTHOS = Fish. The Fish then became a powerful secret symbol identifying members of this new organisation. The Fish symbol has achieved new prominence in modern times.

We find many other associations with fish as a symbol. Peter was a fisherman and a Fish is one of his attributes, as at St Levan. Pisces is a sign of the Zodiac and usually shown as a pair of Fish head to tail. It occurs frequently on Norman archways. The Zodiac is that region of heaven that is nearest to God. Where we find Zodiacal signs we know that we are dealing with Heavenly matters.

At Kirkburn we find the miracle of the loaves and fishes.[11] Medieval theologians saw a parallel between this episode and the distribution of food at the Last Supper. So it gains extra spiritual significance by association with the Host of the pre-

169. St Levan. Corn.
A fish for St Peter; or for us as Christians.

170. Kilpeck. H&W.
Pisces a sign of the Zodiac.

reformation Church.

In Eastern churches they placed the Reserved Sacrament in a model of a Fish whereas in the West they used a Dove.

There is a strong association between Baptism and Fish. New recruits to the Faith appear in this form on several fonts. (see Hinton Parva, p.209)

We often see a mermaid holding a Fish. She is the evil Siren with the Christian soul in her grasp.

Other Fish Shapes.

There was a belief in the Middle Ages that everything on land had a counterpart in the sea. The Bestiary writers describe Bishopfish, Monkfish, Dogfish, Catfish. We find Goatfish, Swanfish and a Horsefish / Sea Horse at Lacock abbey.

The Goatfish is also Capricornus, the Zodiacal sign for Christmas time, the winter solstice and the New Year.

171. Lacock Abbey. Wilts.
A Goatfish.

172. Kirkburn. E.R. Yorks.
The miracle of the loaves and fishes.

Some Fish-like carvings are Dolphins, Whales, a Serra or the Aspidochelone. It can be extremely difficult to distinguish one from another. I have collected examples of each and we can discern a family resemblance for each 'species'. You will find their stories under those headings.

Christians have the Cross for contemplation, but the Fish is their 'attribute.'

[11]. R.W. of 62; Personal Comm.

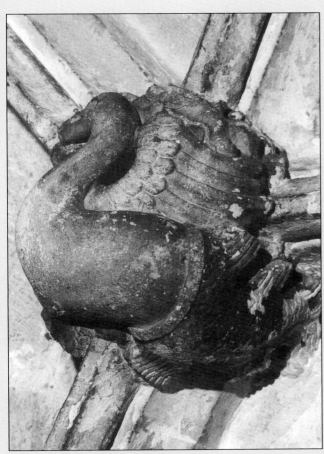

173. Lacock Abbey. Wilts.
A Swanfish.

174. Lacock Abbey. Wilts.
Horsefish or Sea Horse.

FOX

Foxes occur frequently in church carvings, usually running off with a goose and also indulging in other nefarious activities. He is not difficult to recognise. The original Bestiary story is that he liked to lie on his back smeared with red earth while pretending to be dead. Curious birds then land on him to investigate and he immediately seizes them. 'Thus the Devil lies in wait for incautious souls.'

In the Middle Ages there were a whole range of stories about Reynard the Fox and his son Reynardine together with assorted other characters

175. Alne. N.Yorks.
A Fox lying on is back feigning death approached by birds that it will soon catch. See Illust.4. p.93.

176. St Austell. Corn.
A Fox preaching to a gullible lady.

including Noble the Lion, Ysengrin the Wolf, and Tybert the Cat. The stories have the same sort of mocking tone that Brer Rabbit stories do in our day. The Fox was always 'getting away with murder.' We find him carrying off geese; we find him portrayed in priest's cowl and preaching either to a flock of gullible geese or a collection of equally gullible women. The effect achieves an excellent parody on those portrayed. The clergy were jealous of the Friars and their better preaching in the vernacular, so this is most often a dig at the poor and usually not so poor Friars. Some

Foxes die on the gibbet hauled up by geese who have seen the true light. Fig.196.

We can see the ultimate in cynical suavity at Christchurch where a cowled fox surveys his congregation with slit eyes. There is another cynical comment at Beverly St Mary where two Foxes, acolytes to the Priest, each carries a dead goose in their hood.

Occasionally we will see little animal heads and bottoms sticking out of a hill or mound. Some people say that these may be Foxes, others that they are Hares or Conies. They may be reminding us of Matt 8:20. 'Foxes have holes and birds of the air have nests, but the Son of Man has nowhere to lay his head' (Fig.179 The Goat is Christ in this context.) The Vatican Bestiary points out that just as a Fox will enter through one part of his hole and leave by another, so evil ones enter and leave through their treachery and

177. Christchurch. Dorset.
Suave and cynical.

deceptions.[12] In Fig.11 at Ripon, there are the same 'foxes' like those at Forrabury, burrowing in the hill beneath the Antelopes. These are in an evil context, because the Antelope refers to drunkenness. They may complement the thought in the Vatican Bestiary as well as the following idea. The Physiologus (the predecessor to the Bestiary) also says that the Fox injures the earth by burrowing in it; the earth being the man who should bring forth the fruits of righteousness. Sin is the hole that the Devil digs and thereby causes the fruits of the earth to wither away. As King Solomon says 'Take us the foxes, the little foxes that spoil the vines, for our vines have tender grapes.' S. of S. 2.15..

We frequently see carvings of a Fox running off with a goose and being chased by a woman waving a distaff. Some will say that this shows the results of Sloth because the woman should have taken more care. I

178. Padstow. Corn.
A friar preaching to gullible geese.

feel that this may be stretching the intended meaning of the story too far. It is much nearer to the Nun's Priest's Tale of the Cock Chanticleer and the hen Pertelot, as told by Chaucer. The Fox flatters Chanticleer who foolishly lowers his guard with the result that the Fox carries him away. He escapes by flattering the Fox in his turn. The moral at the end of that tale goes; 'For he who wilfully shuts his eyes when he should see, let him never thrive.' The Fox adds 'God give him evil fortune who is so indiscreet as to prate when he should hold his peace.' Chaucer summarises, 'You who hold this tale foolishness, of naught but a fox and a hen, take the moral, good sirs, take the fruit and leave the chaff.'

At Barfrestone there is a Fox like animal playing a harp to an acrobat or dancer. Jugglers, acrobats and women indulging in exhibitionist dancing like Salome were disapproved of by the Church. Animal musicians who encourage such behaviour are manifestations of the devil.

Foxes therefore are nearly always the epitome of treachery.

[12]. Ref 33. p64.

179. Forrabury. Corn.
Possibly Foxes burrowing in the earth so harming it; more likely Hares seeking refuge.

180. Beverley St Mary. E.R.Yorks.
Fox with geese in their hoods act as acolytes to the preacher.

181. Norwich Cathedral.
Domestic chaos. The Fox goes off with the cock. The dog licks the pot;
other pots and dogs in disorder.

Illust. 4.
The Devil lies in wait for incautious souls.

182. Barfrestone. Kent.
A Fox plays the harp for a Salome like dancer.

FROG

Frogs are fairly easy to recognise.

Frogs, perhaps because they are so ugly, carry very negative connotations. Rev.16:13,14. sets the tone. 'And I saw three unclean spirits like Frogs come out of the mouth of the dragon, and out of the mouth of the beast, and out of the mouth of the false prophet. For they are the spirits of devils, working miracles...' Medieval pictures of the Book of Revelation show them coming out of the mouths of demons and from there they have been adopted as an emblem of all that is spiritually unclean.

183. Edlesborough. Bucks.
An evil Frog.

184. Fawsley. N'hants.
Speakers of evil and the spirits of Devils..

94

GARGOYLES

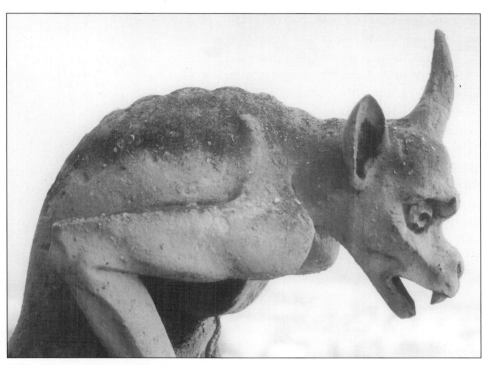

185. Notre Dame. Paris.
A modern gargoyle in the old tradition.

Why did they carve gargoyles? They have always been a puzzle to our literal minds. We can understand them better if we start by erasing our modern concept of evil as an immaterial aspect of mind. We must then make a leap of the imagination and replace that idea with the medieval notion that evil was real and had bodies. These bodies were Devils. Devils and unclean spirits 'lived' in idols; just as they 'lived' in possessed people. Nowadays we would say that such people had epilepsy or one of the more striking forms of mental illness. The Devils took command in the bodies and souls of those that the Church saw as the most obviously sinful. A medieval church contained an array of effigies any of which would make a good home for a Devil. When they consecrated a church the Devils were driven out. They now lived both physically and metaphorically outside the Church as a building and as an institution. Gargoyles personify these devils or illustrate the dreadful sin or fate likely to befall those not within the Church in both senses.

Technically, on many occasions, Gargoyles functioned as water spouts to project rain water away from the building.

186. Fishlake. S.Yorks.
'The devil of a hangover.'

They designed many of them to vomit, pour, even urinate or defaecate, the water onto luckless passers by. In the Somerset area there are a range of non water spout monsters known as Hunky Punks that climb or hang on to the side of the church. At least one will not receive a soaking from these. There really does seem to have been unrestrained artistic licence in the creation of Gargoyles. All the other figures discussed in this book have a long artistic and moral tradition behind them, so that the story they tell is a reinforcement of one already known. Devils as Gargoyles were often *ab initio* creations given form by our worst nightmares but without that same long artistic history behind them. Do not confuse them with the figures that line our Norman corbel tables for they are in a rather

187. Over. Camb.
A vomiting sinner.

different category. Many of these have a warning function. Some warn off devils; some warn of sin; others affirm the goodness in life. They are not strictly Gargoyles at all and so do not fit my initial definition.

188. Evercreech. Som.
A Hunky Punk.

GOAT

To interpret a carving of a goat we first need to decide which variety of goat it is.

The Bestiary recognises two sorts of Goat. It has been a source of endless confusion in our search for the significance of Goat pictures. Each variety has very different natural histories and meanings. We are all aware of the pejorative associations of the phrase 'He is an old goat.' It therefore does not surprise us to find Goats in scenes describing the sin of lust or associated with the devil in a variety of libidinous ways. This is the He-Goat or <u>Hircus</u> of the Bestiary. Hairy, cloven footed, human faced forms with or without horns, that in some respects resemble satyrs, are another development of this satanic Goat image.

Less well recognised but often found in carvings is the mountain goat, <u>Caper</u>. This goat frequented high places and had very keen eyesight. It could tell if the approaching stranger was friend of foe. That is it had the capacity for foresight and omniscience. Such power made it a good symbol for Christ. There are other strands to this story. Ps.104:18 'The high hills are a refuge for the wild Goats and the rocks for conies.' This is the picture at Forrabury. Fig. 179

The Bestiary also points out in the section on Goats that Our Lord refreshes himself in the Church; 'the good works of Christians are his food.' In an

Illust. 5
Wild Goats feed on healing herbs.

189. Exeter Cathedral. Ambulatory.
Goats feed on several varieties of tree.

extension to this theme the Wild Goat that grazed on high pasture fed on Dittany when it was sick. (For those interested, Dittany is Pepperwort, Lepidum Latifolium, one of the Cress family.). The picture of Goats reaching up to feed on herbage was an ancient device adopted from earlier middle eastern civilisations. Artists and therefore carvers use this picture to tell us about the plant that heals. Dittany becomes a poetic equivalent of the Tree of Life that also equates to the Cross and hence to Christ. See the chapter on the Tree of Life for the symbolism becomes very condensed in this area. The Cross is a Tree; a Tree is a Herb, in this case equated with Dittany that has healing properties. We are healed by the Cross. Christ as the goat also feeds on foliage = a Herb composed of the elect in the Church.

The Bestiary adds; 'If preachers are wounded by sin, they run to Christ and are quickly healed.' It is this healing concept that is behind the pictures of Goats feeding on foliage as at Barton-le-Street.

The Scapegoat, that phrase from Old Testament times, refers to the ceremony where the sins of the people are formally laid upon a Goat that is then sent to its fate in the wilderness. Lev.16:9-10. It was part of the ceremony for the Day of Atonement and makes an excellent metaphor for what Christ did for us on the cross. 2 Cor.5:21. 'For he hath made him to be sin for us, who knew no sin.'

Goats also have the meaning of the Lost at the Last Judgement, in the phrase in Matt. 25:32. 'And before him shall be gathered all nations: and he shall separate them one from another, as a shepherd divideth his sheep from the Goats.' I do not have an example from carvings.

There are therefore two very different sets of meanings to draw upon when we find a Goat in a carving; in addition to a host of other associations that we can read about elsewhere.[13] It is tempting to think that lust is the usual one. Undoubtedly a naked lady riding a goat would mean this to us - as a warning. That sort of picture tends to be from a little later in the middle ages than those that show Goats feeding on the Tree of Life. These are commoner in Norman

190. Romsey Abbey. Hants.
A Goat feeds on foliage as Christ feeds on his Church.

carvings and emphasise the healing, wholesome, aspects of a Christian life. We can now see that we have the Goat as Christ who needs the Church for refreshment. We also have the Goat as the Sinner who needs spiritual healing and therefore comes to Christ, in this context foliage or Dittany, in order to achieve a cure.

[13]. Ref 53.

191. Barton-le-Street. N.Yorks.
A Goat feeds on a healing tree.

192. Alne. N.Yorks.
A Goat feeds on healing foliage.

193. Denston. Suff.
A Goat high under the rafters; able to recognise friend or foe from a distance; omniscient like Christ.

194. Tregony/St Cuby. Corn. Font.
A Goat to represent Christ.

195. Widecombe. Devon.
The Scapegoat.

GOOSE

There are few obvious carvings of Geese but many carvings of what could be Geese or Ducks or even Swans. Ducks have no meaning. Swans were famous for their long necks and are easier to identify.

Geese do not appear in the Bible. The Bestiary describes their watchfulness and points out how they saved Rome by their alarm calls. It adds that wild Geese fly high and symbolise those who live far from earthly rank and follow an ordered life. This contrasts with tame Geese who lead a communal life with lots of gossip and slanderous talk. It takes the moral further, saying that if a brother finds negligence and ignorance it is his duty to do something about it.

Geese on their own in carvings are rare and I cannot say for certain that they relate to the above stories. Geese carried off by a fox are common, this being the natural end of those who listen to wily and unworthy preachers.

Geese are part of the stories about St. Martin of Tours who tries to avoid promotion by hiding in the crowd but is given away by some geese. They also feature in stories about St Werburgh who helped to protect villagers' crops against depredations by geese.

196. Bristol Cathedral.
Geese get their own back and hang the Fox.

There was a proverb, 'To shoe the Goose', meaning, whoever meddles in other peoples' affairs is sure to make a mess of them. A modern equivalent is 'Let the shoemaker stick to his last.' We find pictures of it in several places.

BARNACLES or as we would say
BARNACLE GEESE

The Bestiary states that there are *birds* called Barnacles. They grow on trees or logs floating in the water and hold on by their beaks. A shell protects their bodies. When they are big enough they fall off into the water or air and become Barnacle Geese. The whole episode illustrates the principle of the generation of life from inanimate nature, as is the case with the first Adam.

100

'Therefore admire the wonderful ways of the Lord who daily brings forth new creatures without male or female help.'

At Kilpeck two birds hang from what looks like a snake, or it could be a worm. These may be Barnacle Geese hanging from one of the symbols for Earth. For snakes give the appearance of being generated from the earth. The Bestiary also mentions that the Worm is generated

197. Whalley. Lancs.
Shoeing the Goose. 'Whoever meddles in other people's affairs is sure to make a failure of it.'

from wood or any earthy thing. This makes it a good parallel symbol to the Barnacle Geese and therefore appropriate here.

The Bestiary tells us too that bishops and men of religion eat Barnacle Geese during times of fasting without committing sin because they are not flesh nor born of flesh!

198. Kilpeck. H&W.
Possible Barnacle Geese attached to a Worm or a Snake. The sorts of animal that, like Adam, appear to be generated out of earth.

Illust. 6.
Young Barnacle Geese

101

GREEN MAN

The Green Man has for too long been seen mainly as a pagan idol. He appears frequently in virtually every medieval church in situations that are far from pagan and it is time to show that we can receive great positive spiritual messages from this image. The following is a little essay that includes material from the two main books on the subject but with some additional thoughts in outline on how the Green Man fits into a Christian context.

The Green Man is the name coined by Lady Raglan in 1939 to enable us to talk about that enormous number of sculptures where a head appears with foliage. He may peer out of the foliage, or be composed of foliage, or have

199. New Coll. Oxf.
The Green Man.

200. Norwich Cathedral. Cloister.
The Green Man. (God in Nature.)

foliage spewing out the mouth and sometimes the eyes and ears. He also appears in some manuscripts from the Middle Ages but texts rarely refer to him, and then only as the 'leafy one.' Those who wrote on spiritual and theological matters at this time apparently never felt the need to explain his presence. We must assume because it was obviously self-evident. It would be interesting to study separately where and how our loss of understanding has occurred.

Christian symbols in other areas are highly specific if

102

sometimes extremely condensed vehicles of expression. There is no reason why the Green Man should be significantly different. The other symbols gain their authority from the Bible, The Bestiary, Sermons, the Lives of the Saints and other written or well-known sources for authority. We should therefore be careful to take our cues from such authorities and only use our knowledge of 'Art History' to inform that process, not to define it. In that way we shall come to a better understanding of the Green Man in a Christian context.

201. Kilpeck. H&W.
A Norman(Norse) concept of the life giving head. It issues the same foliage as that of the Tree of Life on the adjacent tympanum. Fig.501.

202. Sutton Benger. Wilts.
Christian souls feed on the fruit of the Green Man.

It is tempting to look at 'Art History' for the strands of evidence and bodies of ideas that were probably involved in his evolution. I shall outline some of them later. However we should remember that such a corpus of knowledge was not available to the average patron of a sequence of carvings in a church. For a country church we can envisage the patron being shown a stock book of possible designs for what we might call the fillers or semi-standard ideas that were current in Church furnishing. This would contain Kings, Queens, the Virgin Mary, Christ in Majesty, as well as Bestiary animals and more abstract motifs like Roses, Knots, Spirals and other foliage forms and in particular the Green Man. His form might be chosen from stock. His position and his meaning would certainly be more clearly defined.

Greenness and growth meant something. In a temperate climate such as Europe's we associate it with the burgeoning of new life after the apparent sleep or death of winter. Leaves come forth. Creation comes to life. Gen1:2 'And the Spirit of God moved upon the face of the waters.' Gen 1:11 'and God said, let the earth bring forth grass, the herb yielding seed, and the fruit tree yielding fruit after his kind whose seed is in itself, upon the earth; and it was so.' Gen 1:29 'And God said, behold I have given you every herb bearing seed which is upon the face of the earth, and every tree... Gen 1:31 and God saw everything that He had made, and behold it was very good.' Then later in Gen 3:17. 'Because thou hast hearkened unto the voice of thy wife, and hast eaten of the tree of which I commanded thee, saying, Thou shalt not eat it; cursed is the ground for thy sake, in sorrow shalt thou eat of it all the days of thy life. Thorns and thistles shall it bring forth to thee; and thou shalt eat of the herb of the field.'

So even in Genesis we have the

203. Norwich Cathedral. Cloister.
Christ sporting oak leaves in his hat leads Adam, Eve and all their descendants out of Hell and death.

concepts of Greenness as a blessing, and in contrast Green things that even if not evil may well cause problems.

In Norwich Cathedral cloisters we can see Christ leading souls out the mouth of Leviathan or Hell, and He wears oak leaves upright on his head. (Fig.203). Christ has risen. He invites us to rise with Him. He carries this aura of Greenness for the new life that is available to the redeemed.

In humans, speech is the most favoured means of communication. Without language the whole conceptual frame work of almost everything we do could not exist. To talk about God would be impossible. We should not even have the concept 'God'. How appropriate then that we should have speech shown as leaves issuing from the mouth. Of course these leaves are more than speech. Jn 1:1 'In the beginning was the Word, and the Word was with God, and the Word was God.' (see p.75 for more on Logos.)

Greenness, Foliage, Words and Godhead have become one seamless mode of thinking.

At Brent Knoll the bench ends carry

204. Brent Knoll. Som.
The Church and St John; 'and the Word was God.'

symbols of the Evangelists and of the Pelican, that symbol of Christ shedding his blood for us. Above each roundel is a mitred head from whose mouth issues foliage. Here is a very clear association between the preaching of the Word in earliest Christian times and the then modern times, by the use of foliage to indicate speech and spiritual blessing.

But what about foliage coming from the eyes and ears? It is possible to understand this when one realises that to Medieval Science seeing involved rays coming out of the eyes and, so to speak, lighting up what was around.[14] There was no concept of light or photons emanating from an object. So sight can be as creative as speech and no doubt hearing could be viewed in the same way. If speech creates, and sight creates, it is no wonder that foliage extensions to limbs can also be used to give the same all pervasive, creative meaning. God works through Man.

There are undoubtedly some pretty evil looking Green Men and foliage spewers. I find it impossible to accept that these are

205. Spreyton. Devon.
The Green Man creates His visual world.

pagan; slipped in while the patron was out for the day. Such figures are part of an integral iconography. We may know of pagan antecedents but it does not mean that the same information was available to Medieval theologians. If 'pagan' symbols appear, they have either been given a new meaning (c.f. Lion) or we see them representing the conquered and the defeated. I prefer to see these demonic green forms in the terms of Gen 3:17; the cursed aspect of earth against which Man would have to battle all his life. It was all part of God's original great plan that went so wrong when we acquired the Knowledge of Good and Evil. Maybe these demonic looking Green Men are there to remind us of this fact. Many Green Men with evil looking faces are a Victorian reconstruction or repainting of an earlier

206. Woodbury. Devon.
The gift of hearing.

carving. It may be that they were too enthusiastic in giving the figure a frightening appearance.

If we look outside the Christian tradition for sources from which the Green Man might have evolved we shall not be short of examples. 'Art History' can tell us that Osiris had a green face; that pictures of his consort, Isis, and their son, Horus, are copied almost exactly by Christians wishing to portray Mary holding Jesus on her lap. From Greek mythology we inherit the story of Dionysos who invented wine and

209. Gt. Doddington. N'hants.
The same idea as Fig.210.

**208. Saintes. Charente-Maritime.
Abb. a. Dames.**

A feline mask takes over the function of the Green Man using inspiration via foliage as a metaphor for the third person of the Trinity.

taught the world about agriculture and the arts. He features with grapes and vine leaves, or as a bearded head with a brow covered in ivy. Like Christ he too dies and is reborn, as are many other Gods of ancient times. Our Norse heritage gives us a rich endowment in interlace and knotwork. This can easily become the tendrils and stems of some green foliage and contributes to the general stock of images that influence the way we see and they portrayed, the Green Man.

Our Celtic heritage has given us a veneration for heads. For the Celts the head had the power to protect, to impart prophetic wisdom and to endow the place or the owner with the power that the original person possessed. We also like to give some 'things' human characteristics. We gave the sun and moon faces in very early Medieval times. We still talk of the Man in the Moon. It is natural then to extend this way of thinking to the rest of nature all around us and to give it a face. Maybe the face was God given, maybe sometimes it could be Devil given, but certainly it made a convenient pictorial shorthand to enable one to identify or even identify with... 'Nature.'

106

The Cross was known as, 'the Tree', on which Christ died, and many carvings and pictures show the Cross with stubs of branches up the trunk and even leaves from the Cross arms. The Cross in the early medieval glass at Chartres and Bourges is coloured green in that other dimension of Christian story telling.

These and many more (see foliage under Goat) are part of the body of ideas that permeate our thinking and some of them may have formed the 'obvious' background knowledge of our forbears. They might have found it difficult to identify or particularise any of it. However aspects of this heritage and folk memory would certainly have helped them to feel comfortable with a picture of the Green Man.

We find a face giving forth vines laden with grapes in many places. Jn15:5 'I am the Vine, you are the branches'; said Christ. Green Men join Kings and Queens in the most favoured places above the altars at the East End of our churches. Green Men are frequent in Lady Chapels as if guarding and influencing for good the foetus the Virgin will carry.

In the sense that we are all made in the image of God yet are all different, so too the Green Man may be a spiritual image with as many facets as there are human beings to comprehend him. We do, after all, find him most often in a Christian context. We find him virtually everywhere in our Western civilisation. He is so universal and so emotionally powerful that we should also benefit from all the other modes of understanding that come via scholarship and poetry.[15]

209. Much Marcle. H&W.
Nature created and sustained.

210. Crowcombe. Som.
The Green Man utters the Vine. A direct reference to Christ who says, 'I am the Vine.'

[14]. Ref 63.

[15]. See Ref 7.

GRIFFINS

Griffins or Gryphons, have the forepart of an eagle and the hind part of a lion. Do not confuse them with Dragons or Wyverns who may look very similar. Griffins carry two sets of quite different meanings so context is all important when trying to understand them. Historically they came from the East, where they were the finders and guardians of treasure.

They were so large and ferocious that one could carry off an ox, and if they met a man they would tear him to pieces. They were the sworn enemies of horses. Their good qualities stem from their

211. Ripon. N.Yorks.
A Griffin tears a man to pieces.

212. Chester Cathedral.
A Griffin guards the body of a fallen knight.

guardian abilities. They guard the corpse of the fallen knight. They guard the Tree of Life. Dante used the Griffin as a symbol of Christ. 'For He had the strength and nobility of the Lion the King of Beasts, plus the vision and the ability to soar like an Eagle.'

One of the legends about Alexander tells how he harnessed two griffins to a basket and, by tempting them with meat stuck on the ends of poles, persuaded them to lift him up to the heavens from where he could survey the earth. This episode accounts for most of the carvings that illustrate the Alexander romances. They are all about Pride.

(See under Fables for a fuller account.)

Many and fearsome are the other stories attached to Griffins, a part of our general heritage of stories from the East. This can make it difficult to feel the message the carver intended. The nearest we may get on many occasions is that they can both do good service and be violently dangerous. They merit respect.

213. Beverley St Mary. E.R. Yorks.
Two Griffins guard the Tree of Life where Conies seek refuge.

214. Carlisle. Cumb.
A Griffin preens to show regeneration and renewal.

109

GRYLLES OR NO-BODIES

The margins of Medieval manuscripts provide a rich source for little figures called Grotesques, Nondescripts, Grylles or NoBodies. They are composite forms, usually of a head joined to deformed legs with no body in between, or variations on this theme. They appear to be skilfully executed doodles but the carvers took some of them for their models and we now have a wide variety in our churches. Nobody, figuratively both 'No Body' and metaphorically 'as not worthy of consideration', is probably the best description with a moral perspective. In the Middle Ages they had the pejorative sense of Lost Souls, the folk for whom there really was no hope. (Artistically they have a long history, occurring on Summerian and Cretan seals and gemstones from 2000 to 1500 BC. The experts of the early Middle

215. Norwich Cathedral. Cloisters.
Grylles, or just grotesques?

Ages thought that they could not have been carved by human hand and must therefore hold magical power. Such magical power may account, in part, for why the designs were so popular in the margins of medieval manuscripts.)

There is an alternative explanation for some of them in a book published by Caxton, The Pilgrimage of the Sowle. 1483. In it he describes the Worm of Conscience who appears as a witness for Satan. He is hideous, toothless and with no body but only a tail. The teeth wear away with the endless biting that Conscience inflicts upon the Soul, all to no avail.[16] Caxton's ideas are really too late to be the source for the carvings although he may be reflecting current received wisdom on the subject. We may therefore have two sharply contrasted possible meanings for the carvings and I find it impossible to distinguish one from the other.

216. Wordwell. Suff.
The Worm of Conscience?

[16]. Ref 59.

217. Tewkesbury. Gloucs.
Lost Souls.

218. Ufford. Suff.
No-Bodies.

219. New Coll. Oxf.
Grylle or grotesque?

111

HARE and also see Rabbit

We are probably better acquainted with Rabbits than with Hares. We might easily conclude that all the carvings of these sorts of animals are indeed Rabbits, but we would be mistaken; for they are probably all Hares. The Bible recognises Conies that could refer to either while the Bestiary only mentions Hares and it is Hares that have many different stories to tell us.

The Bestiary describes Hares as timid creatures who fear God

220. Lower Swell. Gloucs.
A Hare on the chancel arch seeks shelter in the rock of Christ.

221. Bishop Wilton. E.R.Yorks.
David with his sling slays Goliath while two Hares (ourselves) await deliverance from the hand of the Philistine.

and who put their trust not in themselves but in their Creator. Ps. 104:18. 'The high hills are a refuge for the hedgehogs and the rocks for Hares.' (Vulg.). So when we see two Hares in association with David smiting Goliath, as at Bishop Wilton, the carvings are probably there to remind us that Christ, like the rocks, is our refuge. David, who was an Old Testament 'type' of Christ, slew Goliath (Satan) and saved the watching army of Israelites. David in faith and confidence states 'The Lord that delivered us out of the paw of the lion and out of the paw of the bear will deliver us out of the hand of the Philistine.' 1 Sam:17:37.

Nowadays we are more likely to associate the Hare with the moon, and with being madly overactive in March. The Middle Ages thought of the Hare as having uninhibited mating behaviour just as we associate Rabbits with being oversexed and overfertile. They also thought that the Hare could conceive while still pregnant. These are the sources for the association with lust, libido and sex and with being bewitched.

There are other associations. These include the idea of it having excellent hearing if poor eyesight. It could also be hermaphrodite, that is male and female in the one body; as well as being able to conceive without the male. The last idea meant that it could be Virginal, and that is how it became an attribute of the Virgin Mary.

The name 'hare' sounds like 'whore' that makes it suitable for lewd word play. It is also an attribute of Cowardice; as such it joins the Snail and they often appear

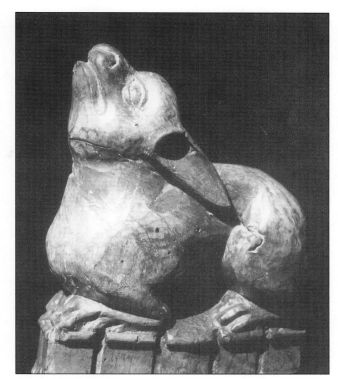

222. Denston. Suff.
A Hare looks at the moon and the Queen of Heaven.

together in the margins of illustrated Medieval manuscripts. A man terrified of a Hare features in one of the little carvings on the south portal of Chartres cathedral. Unfortunately the Hare has quite worn away.

The idea in most situations is likely to be one of three. In early Norman work, it is the timid Christian seeking refuge in Christ. Later, the single Hare is likely to carry a libidinous connotation, or to symbolise the exact opposite, the Virgin Mary. Context and position will give one the clues.

The Hawk pouncing on a Hare, which is a common finding, is using

223. Wells Cathedral.
A Hare; for the Virgin Mary?

an ancient picture with a world-wide distribution. In a Christian context it describes the defeat of lust, the Hare, by Christ the Eagle or Hawk. Fig.227.

Easter Hares, an interesting sidelight.

A curious by-product of the sexual association has produced the edible, usually chocolate, Easter Hare. Hares were ritually eaten to gain their 'strength' at certain spring festivals of the Greeks and Romans. Pliny said that the eater of the Hare acquires sexual attractiveness for nine days. It seems probable that from such pagan habits; when combined with the spring festival that we now call Easter, there evolved the association of an eaten Hare with an eaten Eucharist; for both should provide 'strength' in their different ways. We now eat the Hare entirely as a sweet the other aspects we have totally

224. Chartres. Eure et Loir.
The knight drops his sword and runs in terror from a Hare. Cowardice, a result of sin.

suppressed.[17]

'**Tinners' Rabbits**', so common on West Country roof bosses, probably have nothing to do with Tinners. They are a clever visual image with three Hares sharing ears. The earliest known example is in a Buddhist monastery on the Chinese border from the 5th or 6th Century. These images are widespread both in England and on the Continent, and sometimes there are four Hares not three. (As in an illustration in a Bestiary. MS Bodley.764.Ref. 8.) So why did West Country carvers choose three Hares for their churches? We do not know. We can surmise that they are a symbol of the Trinity. We could suppose that they are Hares seeking refuge in the rock of Christ; or we can look at them in a totally unrelated and possibly more profitable way. We can explore the great significance that number had in

225. Forrabury. Corn.
Hares or conies seek refuge in the high hills where the Goat (Christ) feeds, and surveys all.

the medieval scheme of things. Three was the number of Completion; of beginning, middle and end. Six was a perfect number. The individual soul in the Christian and Neo-Platonic philosophy that the Church embraced, moved out of the 'world' soul, to a home in this earthly life, to a final reintegration with the 'world' soul. This third stage, the return of the soul to God, was the high point of an earthly life; the End in time and in aspiration. Here perfection and the number six could be symbolically equivalent.[18]

226. Ilsington. Devon.
'Tinners Rabbits.' Either the Trinity, or a state of perfection that may be attained at the end of an earthly life?

It is this line of thinking that may give us a better clue to the 'meaning' of Tinners Rabbits where there are three Rabbits linked by three ears in a perfectly integrated circle.

We find other symbols of soul journeys, such as the spiral, on roof bosses in the same and nearby churches. Here there is no beginning, middle or end, just a completeness, a wholeness, a final integration with the Divine. Far fetched? Maybe. However the medieval mind sought interpretation at four levels and could think 'poetically' far more easily than we can with our 'scientific' training.

There is also this final thought from the Middle Ages. 'Just as a Serpent stands for the Devil, the Hare stands for the quick course of human life.'[19]

227. Wilby. Suff.
An Eagle kills the Hare. The defeat of Lust.

[17]. Ref 53.

[18]. Ref 30.

[19]. Ref 61.

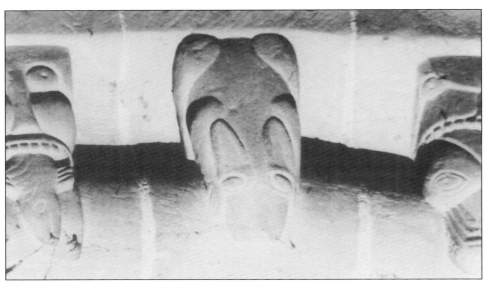

228. Adel. W.Yorks.
Chancel arch. A hare seeks or has found salvation.

229. Reepham. Norf.
A supplicant Hare.

HARPY

The Harpy was a mythical creature with the head and breasts of a woman and the wings and body of a bird like a Vulture.

Harpies are few and far between, which may be just as well since they have such a fearsome reputation. Our current understanding that Harpy means a rapacious woman may not be far from the Medieval meaning. The Harpy, because it was the tormentor of Misers in Greek myth, was the attribute of Avarice, one of the Seven Deadly Sins. In classical antiquity Harpies were male or female birds of prey that snatched food

230. New Coll. Oxf.
A Harpy, so beautiful yet so evil.

231. Cheriton Bishop. Devon.
A Harpy or a Lamia.

from the table and fouled what they could not eat. Both sexes appear in our carvings.

The male Harpy at Gorran is interesting because it accompanies a triple faced crowned head below it. It is tempting to see such triple faces as meaning the Trinity; but in many cases they refer to the prince of Hell, one of the 'the Infernal Rulers.' We find a similar crowned three-in-one head on a 'Tallage' roll of 1233 where it represents the then richest Jew in England as the King of the Demons in Hell.[20] So this pairing is probably not at all accidental but a direct allusion to avarice wherever we might find it.

The Harpy, (or Lamia) at Cheriton Bishop may, in a rather indirect way, be warning against prostitution. Prostitutes take a man's wealth, a cause of loss to him and of course to the Church and so attract the epithet; avaricious.

[20]. Ref 5.

117

232. Ludlow. Shrops.

A Harpy all smiles in her hennin but all evil in reality.

233. Gorran. Corn.

A male Harpy associates with the King of the Usurers prince of Hades.

234. Clayhanger. Devon.

An evil, serpent tailed form.

Hart Stag Deer

They are fairly easy to recognise, because they generally have branched horns.

Unusually for the Middle Ages, the stories about Stags all carry positive applications. 'As the Hart panteth after the water brooks, so panteth my soul after thee O God.' Ps 42:1. This quotation and the famous hymn based upon it are probably the only real allusions to Deer that spring

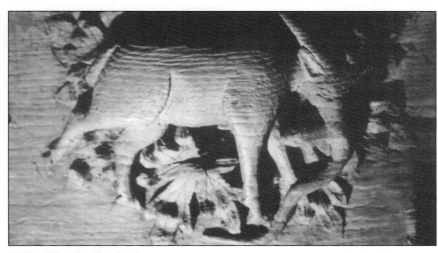

235. Ely Cathedral.
The Hart eats the Serpent. Christ kills Satan.

236. Melbury Bubb. Dorset.
A Hart feeds on the healing plant, the Tree.

to mind when faced with an obvious Stag in a carving. The Bestiary adds to the story in two ways. The Stag, if ill, sought a cure by eating a serpent as well as by eating Dittany. Additionally the Stag hunted the fiery serpent and in the chase became so heated by the serpent's breath that it had to find a stream to slake its thirst. The Stag fills its stomach with water in order to disgorge it down the serpent's hole. This forces out the serpent, which it can now easily kill. The good Stag that conquers the evil Serpent is a metaphor for Christ's actions on earth.

In an extra elaboration the writers point out that when Deer seek better pasture on the far side of a river, they will help each other across as they swim. They do this by proceeding in line ahead with each one resting his chin on the rump of the one in front. There is a delightful picture of this at Bishops Lydeard and I think the animal up to his haunches in 'water' at Eynesbury refers to the same story. The Bestiary makes the parallel with those members of Holy

Church who would leave this world and its pleasures because they prefer the pastures of heaven. The 'more perfect' help the weaker brethren by example and good works. Similarly if they find a place of sin, they leap over it at once. The rare picture of a leaping deer refers to this endeavour.

The Hunt where dogs surround a Stag has yet another meaning. The Stag is Christ and the dogs are Satan. (But see under Dog).

A young Fawn is a symbol of Christ. This derives from the beautiful allegory in the Song of Songs. 2:9. 'My beloved is like a roe or young Hart.'

Sometimes we find carvings of St Hubert and St Eustace accompanied by Deer. In both cases the Deer will have a cross between the antlers. These are Christian

237. Bishops Lydeard. Som.
Deer follow each other across the stormy river of life to better pasture in the kingdom of heaven.

versions of the stories told by the Celts in pre-Christian times, when to slay a Deer was to ensure some magical happening, or the receipt of a significant vision. Deer also accompany St Giles because one befriended him in the forest.

So a solitary Stag is likely to mean either Christ himself or the faithful person seeking salvation in Christ. The fact that Deer shed their antlers that then regrew adds to the general picture of regeneration and renewal. Besides eating serpents when sick, Deer also seek out Dittany. The healing property of Dittany merges with aspects of the Tree of Life story and therefore with The Cross. (See Goat). They extend the metaphor in some Bestiaries[21] so that

238. Eynesbury. Hunts.
A Deer swims the river.

Christ is the water that the Stag drinks. The Christian is renewed just as the Stag is renewed at the fountain of cool, healing water.[22]

The pleasant picture of a Hart browsing on foliage, such as we see at Bishops Lydeard, comes to mean much more than just the quarry of the chase. It is the Christian eating of the Tree of Life and being healed. The Serpent is dead. The Faithful can help

239. Godmanchester. Cambs.
'My beloved is like a roe or young deer.'

each other through the difficulties of this world to more fruitful pastures where 'streams of living water flow.'

[21]. Ref 23.

[22]. Ref 58.

240. Bishops Lydeard. Som.
A Hart in the Tree of Life.

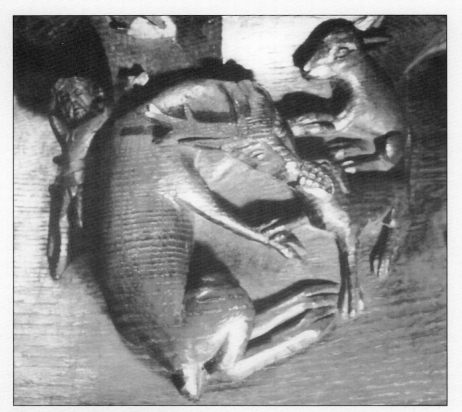
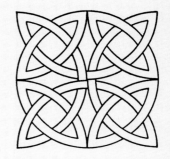

241. Coventry. Holy Trinity.
A Stag beset by hounds; Christ beset by evil.

242. Elkstone. Gloucs.
Three corbels tell the story of Christ attacked by Satan.

HAWK

One feels that with Hawks and hawking the intention of the carver should be clear, but this is far from the case. They are easy to recognise although eagles and vultures might cause confusion.

Pictures of Hawking, a sport of the nobility, illustrate the month of May in books of Hours. In these books we find pictures of a series, 'The Labours of the Months.' These labours were often paired with the signs of the Zodiac, and used to compare and contrast the earthly and heavenly cycles. A Hawk seizing prey, usually the Hare, is an ancient motif taken into Christian story depicting the elimination of undue sexuality (the Hare) by Christ (the Hawk)

243. Stowlangtoft. Suff.
Christ the Hawk seizes Lust the Hare.

The Hawk seizing a bird is possibly a misrepresentation of a Hawk seizing a Quail for this is the picture in the Bestiary accompanying the chapter on Quails. There the writer tells us that a Hawk seizes the leader of a flock of Quails when they approach land after crossing the sea. Land is earthly pleasure; the Hawk is the Devil who seizes those who seek earthly things out of greed. The rest of the flock cross the sea of this world to the love of God. The moral; everyone should chase a good leader and not one dedicated just to his own ends.

To confuse the image yet further the Hawk, says one Bestiary, is the image of the Holy person who seizes the kingdom of God. It then quotes Job 39:26. 'Does the Hawk fly by thy (i.e.Job;s) wisdom and stretch her wings towards the south?' Then it tells us

that however intelligent or conscientious we may be the Holy Spirit will stretch us still further. We shall cast off old feathers in order to fly with new ones. (The Ibis has a similar spiritual story.)

Among the tools of hawking, the fetterlock, besides having an heraldic association (House of York), can mean the confinement and discipline inherent in a monk's life. A Hawk when confined in the mews loses old feathers and puts on new. So a monk would put off old vices and adorn himself with the clothes of the new man. The Hawk returning to his lure was the monk returning to his convent after journeying in the world. Preachers make use of the whole training of Hawks as a metaphor for the righteous life that people should follow. The Hawk, they remind us, when tame is gentle yet still keeps plundering other birds. In the same way there are people who seem to be gentle and good but in reality are in league with wicked individuals.

There is a special story attached to a Hawk or Eagle holding a swaddled baby - The Lathom Legend - that is relevant to that family from the NW of England. In this an Eagle carries off the child but it grows up to inherit the family title. In more general terms an Eagle carrying off another animal or a baby is said to represent Judgement.

244. Ludlow. Shrops.
A Hawk and fetterlocks. The discipline of the monastic life and etc.

245. Ponts-de-Cé. Maine et Loir.
The Hawk seizes a bird; possibly an analogy for the Hawk taking the leading Quail. 'Do not follow the self seeker.'

HEDGEHOG

There are only a few Hedgehogs in church carvings and they are easy to recognise. The even rarer Porcupine probably shares the symbolism because the Bestiary does not give them a special chapter. In all those that I have come across they mean the Devil. In the Bestiary story the Hedgehog stole grapes from the vine letting them fall to the ground. Then he would roll on them so that they became impaled on his prickles and carried them off home to his young. This shows that he is full of vice and prepared to cheat others of the fruits of their labours. However even the Bestiary admits that

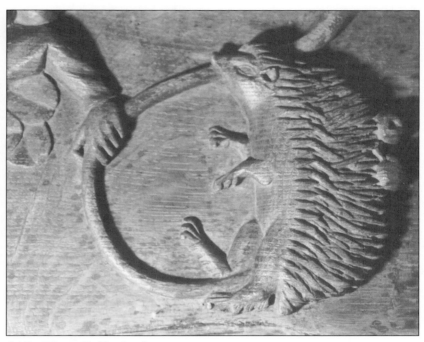

246. New Coll. Oxf.

A Hedgehog has stolen some grapes; the fruit of other men's labours.

247. Barfrestone. Kent.

A Hedgehog; part of a series of evildoers.

one can give this a favourable interpretation. The Hedgehog was being prudent on behalf of his young.

In Ps.104:18. Vulgate version. 'The high hills are a refuge for Hedgehogs and wild Hares.' The rock of the 'high hills' is Christ where Hedgehog and Hare are suppliant sinners seeking refuge. In the King James version they translate 'Hedgehog' as wild goat. This makes more sense to us for there are many pictures of goats climbing but there are some carvings in France that may owe their meaning to the Vulgate version.

248. Childrey. Oxon.

A Hedgehog takes some grapes so is attacked by a faithful hound.

249. Cartmel. Cumb.

A Porcupine or Hedgehog.

126

HERON and check with Crane

Herons, storks and cranes are all long necked birds with a crest so that identification may be difficult.

The Heron, says the Bestiary, is an example of that ideal person whose soul rejoices in the eternal. At the same time his life is sustained by this transitory world. The Bestiary adds that because it flies so high it was a symbol of the souls of the elect. Because it builds a nest in trees but feeds on water it is an example of the just person taking nourishment from fleeting things but placing his hope (that is his young), in sublime matters. It states that they fly above all tempests to the serenity of heaven where they may behold the countenance of God.

Sometimes the writers' descriptions confuse Herons with Storks and Cranes. Different Bestiaries may have pictures where the artist either has not known the difference, or out of idleness used any long necked bird picture for any one of the three. So the carvers, who took their models from the pictures in the Bestiaries, may well confuse us by their attempts at naturalism. Nevertheless each has its own little story and we can benefit from the variety of instruction. Please look under Crane for the tales.

250. Gt. Gransden. Cambs.
A Heron rejoicing in the eternal.

HOOPOE

Hoopoes are difficult to recognise and it is easier to identify them by a process of elimination. They are one of only five birds with crests. The others are the crane, the peacock, the stork, and sometimes the phoenix. These others all have other significant characteristics such as long legs or a large tail that should make them easy to eliminate from the list of possibilities.

'The Hoopoe is a horrid bird', begins the Bestiary writer; influenced by that bird's habit of frequenting dunghills where it finds a plentiful supply of food. We

251. Carlisle. Cumb.
Hoopoe young tend their ageing parent.

see it as a particularly beautiful bird but this was not one of the writer's considerations. In spite of his initial derogatory tone the writer goes on to praise the Hoopoe family behaviour. The young take great care of their ageing parents. They pluck out the old feathers and care for the eyes. In this they set an excellent example. They say that if so horrid a bird can take such good care of mother and father, then how much better should a Christian be able to care for his or her parents. They quote Ex.20:12 & 21:17. 'God commanded that men should honour father and mother.'

252. Gt. Gransden. Cambs.
Hoopoe with eggs.

253. St Levan. Corn.
A pair of Hoopoes?

Illust. 7
The young attend a Hoopoe parent.

254. Reepham. Norf.
Possibly a Hoopoe.

129

HORSE

There should be no difficulty in recognising a horse in carving.

The Bestiary, although it has a long essay on the Horse, gives it no moral qualities nor does it give us any lesson. It does give the Horse some characteristics that may have been significant for the carvers. They can scent battle. *They can recognise their masters.* The sound of the trumpet encourages them to fight. If one cuts off the manes of mares they will lose their desire for mating. The Bible points out the strength and courage of Horses in Job.39.

In popular folklore everywhere there is a strong phallic component to all stories about Horses and we preserve this in Horse related words such as riding for intercourse.

Thus it happens that in the Middle Ages the Horse could be a symbol for the sinner or sexual appetites. In the Psychomachia of Prudentius (circa AD400) a poem about the battle between Virtues and Vices, Pride and Lust mount unruly steeds who promptly throw them. We often see Pride falling off a Horse. It is less common to find Lust doing so.

The Normans had isolated Horses heads in the corbel tables of their Romanesque churches. There are Horses heads all round the window arch of some churches in SW France, for example Perignac. There are Horses or Horse like animals on the bench ends of East Anglian churches. What do they all mean? The ones on bench ends, I do not know. The ones on the corbel tables especially if near the east end are most likely to be an image of the Christian ready and waiting for his Master as He approaches. The one from Studland is certainly very alert. Alternatively they might be warning devils to flee. In the OED[23] it mentions under apotropaic, which roughly means to warn off evil, that Horses heads were used with an apotropaic intention on some buildings in Rome. The Norsemen believed that to hold out towards the enemy the severed head of a Horse would have a fatal effect on the opponent.[24] Other figures on the same corbel tables certainly have a warning intent. It may not be unreasonable to assume that these heads do the same though I do not know of a written authority for such an idea. The rear half of a Horse impaled by a portcullis tells of the story of Sir Yvain. For details see under 'Fables'.

[23]. Ref 47.

[24]. Ref 14.

255. Stowlangtoft. Suff.
A Horse with uncertain meaning.

256. Studland. Dorset.
An alert Horse awaiting the Master's return.

257. Chartres. Eure et Loir.
'Pride goes before a fall.'

HUNTER and also see Boar and Centaur

To be the Hunter or to be hunted are common themes that we can all understand.

The Hunter in carving is usually Christ or the Good Christian conquering the sinner or his sins. In some places we find the roles reversed. Satan is the Hunter lying in wait, ever ready to pounce on the unwary or those that have strayed. It is usually not difficult to decide which is which and our appreciation

258. Alphington. Devon.
Christ the hunter slays the evil serpent.

259. Hereford Cathedral.
The Christian hunter with his Cross spears Satan as a Boar.

will be all the deeper when we have digested and absorbed the stories presented by the writers of the Bestiary.

HYDRA

The Hydra, not on any account to be confused with the Hydrus, is a beast from Greek mythology. It had nine heads. Hercules had to kill it in his second labour. For every head that he cut off another two would grow as substitutes; finally he overcame it with fire.

Rev 17:3. 'and I saw a woman sit upon a scarlet coloured beast, full of names and blasphemy, having

260. New Coll. Oxf.

A Hydra of five of the seven deadly sins; accompanied by one man beating himself in penance while the devil leaves another through an act of exorcism.

261. Norwich Cathedral. Cloisters.

The beast with seven heads and ten horns.

seven heads and ten horns.' The carvers use this happy coincidence of Greek myth with Bible story very rarely. On a misericord in the chapel at New College Oxford there is a five or six headed beast representing the seven deadly sins. The supporters show on one side a man scourging himself in sorrow for his bad behaviour while on the other side there is a man receiving absolution as the Devil leaves his body.

We can also see the Revelation episode in Norwich Cathedral cloisters where it is one of a whole series relating to the Apocalypse.

HYDRUS

In carvings we recognise the Hydrus as a smooth, occasionally fluted, round or elongated shape in or near the mouth of some potentially fierce creature.

The Hydrus of the Bestiary is a water snake and is the enemy of the crocodile. The Hydrus sees a crocodile basking with its mouth open. It rolls itself into a ball, covers itself with mud and slips down the crocodile's throat unnoticed. Once inside it could eat away at the

262. Topsham. Devon. Font.
The Crocodile swallows the Hydrus. The prelude to the death of Satan.

263. Stone. Bucks. Font.
The Hydrus slips down the Crocodile's throat.

intestines, killing the crocodile and emerge unharmed.

The Hydrus or Idrus is an insignificant animal in the Bestiary but we find that they used the story extensively in sculpture. Because it is so insignificant and few people know it we run the risk of denying ourselves the benefit of the potent spiritual doctrine to which it alludes.

The Bestiary makes the Hydrus a picture of Christ, who puts on human flesh, and who descends into Hell after the crucifixion. The Apostles' creed makes the same statement. Once He is in Hell Christ binds Satan; effectively destroying him. This is the story that we find in Revelation and in the Apocryphal Gospels. Christ returns leading Adam, Eve, the Patriarchs and Prophets and all those who had died before this time. (See item on Harrowing of Hell.). The story is that of the end of Satan and the freeing of humanity and therefore the individual from the terrors of the results of sin.

We find the Hydrus on fonts for baptism can initiate our salvation. We find it at the entrances to churches and in the church itself. It reminds us about the thoroughness of Christ's victory over evil.

I give a range of examples to show the wide variety of forms the interpretation of this story can take. Be suspicious of 'large tongues', they may be the Hydrus. It can appear as an ovoid with spiral markings or as a ball with no markings at all. If the 'ball' has facial markings then the animal concerned is likely to be either a Hyena or a 'Disgorging Monster', a personification of the great deep. (See

264. Lakenheath. Suff.
The Hydrus slips down the Crocodile's throat.

p.154. under Leviathan.)

Church carvers retell the same basic story hundreds of times in pictures of Samson rending the jaws of a lion and of David also killing a lion. (Lincoln, Stretton Sugwas.) Fig.276, 316. Actual pictures of the Harrowing of Hell come in earlier carvings as at Quenington. Later carvings express the idea rather differently. The Triumphant banner of Christ, the Vexillum, stands above the head of Leviathan or accompanies an open tomb. There are other Old Testament stories known as 'Types' that are presentiments of this great feat. They are the stories of David versus Goliath, Daniel in the Lion's den, and Moses leading the children of Israel out of Egypt.

See **Harrowing of Hell.** p.139.

265. Kilpeck. H&W.
The Hydrus slips down the Crocodile's throat.

266. Bristol Cathedral.
Choir stalls. The Hydrus slips down the Crocodile's throat.

267. Dinton. Bucks.
The Hydrus enters the Crocodile's throat. St Michael slays the Serpent. (See note 3)

136

268. Tissington. Derbys.
A Crocodile about to swallow the Hydrus.

269. Bristol. St Mary Redcliffe
Crocodile and Hydrus.

270. York. St Margaret's, Walmgate. W.Door.
A Crocodile faces the Hydrus.

271. Adel. W.Yorks.
A Crocodile head swallows the Hydrus.

272. Stoke Dry. Rutl.
N. pillar to chancel. The Crocodile swallows the Hydrus just below a Lion uttering Life giving foliage.

HARROWING OF HELL

It is one of those phrases that many of us have heard, yet most of us nowadays are unaware of the full story. The Harrowing of Hell tells of the triumphant expedition of Christ when, after His Crucifixion; He brought away from Hades the souls of the righteous who had died and been held captive since the beginning of time.[25] The story was well known by the 2nd Century and occurs in several Latin and Greek versions. It

273. Quenington. Gloucs.
Christ spears and binds Satan, then leads Adam and other souls out of the mouth of Hell.

274. Thorpe Arnold. Leics.
Daniel safe between two Lions. c.f. Fig.319.

was popular right through the Middle Ages, and so many of our carvings allude to it that a short version here might be appropriate.

There are good accounts in the Golden Legend and the Apocryphal Gospel of Nicodemus on which the Golden Legend is based. This is a much shortened version that I hope retains the atmosphere of the originals.[26]

Annas and Caiaphas and Pilate hear stories that Jesus has been seen since the crucifixion with a great multitude of people who are only visible to certain individuals. There are two particular people in this multitude, Karinus and Leucius. Annas and Caiaphas ask them to tell how they were raised from the dead. They indicate that they cannot speak but will describe it all in writing. This is their story...

We were in Hell in darkness when suddenly there was a great light and Hell did tremble. Isaiah says that the light is the light of the Father about which he, Isaiah, prophesied: 'The people that walked in darkness have seen a great light, and now it has come and shone upon us that sit in death.' Then there comes a great voice, from the Son of the Most High Father. 'Draw back, O Princes, your gates; remove your everlasting doors; Christ the Lord, the king of glory approacheth to enter in.' Satan comes to tell his minions to shut the gates, to put in place bars of iron, and prepare to fight. This they do with great howlings while the people rejoice.

Then John the Baptist appears to say that this is the Lamb of God, the Son of God, the Dayspring from on High, that will

275. Barming. Kent.
Christ leads Adam and Eve out of Hell.

276. Stretton Sugwas. H&W.
Samson or David rends a Lion.

visit us that sit in darkness and the shadow of death.

Satan suggests to Hell, who is both a person and a place, that he should get ready to receive Him. Hell retorts with the thought that the voice was that of the Son of God, and that therefore all his bonds are now wide-open. He should not be let in lest they too will be taken captive by Him.

There is, at this point, a little story

about Adam who tells Seth his son to recount to the patriarchs and prophets all that he has heard from Michael the Archangel. Adam reminds Seth that when Adam was dying he sent Seth to the gates of Paradise to ask for the Oil of Mercy. Michael replies to this request by saying that Adam could not have the oil for 5500 years till the Son of God came to earth to raise up the body of Adam and the dead.

Adam now says to Satan that the Lord is coming and that he will

277. Bristol Cathedral.
Samson, sporting the jaw bone of an ass, rends the Lion's jaws.

be captured and bound until the end of the world. Satan orders Hell to make ready to receive Jesus who boasts he is the Son of God, when really he is only a man that fears death as He said, 'My soul is sorrowful unto death.' He has always been Satan's enemy. For instance all the blind, lame, deaf, dumb and possessed have been healed with a word. To which Hell responds by asking what sort of person is this Jesus who though he fears death, still purports to resist Satan's power? If he is so mighty in the human side to his nature, then in his godly form no one will be able to withstand his power. Satan, Prince of Tartarus, replies, do not worry; I have stirred up the Jews against him. I have speared him and given him gall and vinegar to drink, and prepared a cross to crucify him. Hell asks if he is the same man who raised Lazarus because, if so, he is going to be such a strong God that he will set everyone free.

Meanwhile David

278. Eardisley. H&W.
Christ seizes Adam by the right hand to lead him out of Hell.

and Jeremiah both tell of the prophecies that they made when they were upon earth. Everyone rejoices in the light of the Lord. Satan tries to get out but could not do so because Hell had fenced him in on every side. His minions tease him saying 'Why are you so afraid?'

There is another cry of; 'Lift up, O Princes, your gates and be ye lift up ye everlasting doors and the King of Glory shall come in.' Satan and Hell cry out, 'Who is this King of Glory?' Answers the Lord's voice, 'The Lord strong and mighty in battle.' There then appears one of the robbers bearing a cross who asks for admittance. Satan lets him in. He shines brightly. He tells how he was a robber crucified beside Christ and that he is only just ahead of the Lord Jesus who is

279. Poughill. Corn.
The Flag of Victory beside a head appearing from Hell's mouth.

280. Launcells. Corn.
The Cross and Flag of Victory over the mouth of Hades.

immediately following. David and all the saints demand that the gates be opened.

Suddenly Hell quakes, the gates of death with their locks are broken. All things are a laid open. Satan stands forlornly in the middle all cast down. Christ enters carrying a chain with which he binds the neck of Satan, casts him backwards into Tartarus and putting his holy foot on Satan's throat and says; 'Today I deliver thee unto eternal fire.' Jesus calls Hell and commands him to hold Satan until 'the day that I command thee.' He is cast into the bottomless pit.

Then the Lord greets Adam; 'Peace be unto you and all your children.' All the saints gather together. The Lord seizes Adam by the right hand, but Adam goes on his knees to the Lord. He asks that, just as He has set up the Cross for a token of Redemption on earth, so please Lord to set the Cross as a sign of Victory in and over Hell, that death may have no more dominion. So it was done. All went out of there and left Satan and Hell in Tartarus.

The Lord goes holding Adam by the hand whom he delivers to Michael to take to Paradise. There they meet Enoch, who was 'translated'; Elias the Thesbite who went up in a chariot of fire and the other robber to whom it was promised that today he be with Christ in Paradise.

Karinus and Leucius say that that is as much as they are allowed to tell. They are suddenly transfigured.

Quenington. Fig.273. Christ tramples on a bound Satan and spears him. Adam and Eve and another figure rise out of the mouth of a monster. At Bristol and Stretton Sugwas there is the picture of Samson rending the lion's jaws. Note Samson's jawbone of an ass with which he has recently slain a thousand men. Judg.15:16. A head

281. St Newlyn East. Corn.
The chains of Hell and Hell's mouth.

282. Dinton. Bucks. Tympanum.
Two animals feed on the Tree of Life. Below; The Crocodile swallows the Hydrus and St Michael kills the Serpent. (Note 3)

between two lion's heads probably refers to Daniel in the lion's den. These are both Old Testament 'Types' or stories that were seen as forerunners to the great event of the death of Satan and the deliverance of mankind from the power of evil.

[25] . Ref 52 p278.

[26] . Ref 37;57.

143

HYENA

Hyenas are difficult to recognise and indeed we may only do so where an animal eats a corpse or a bone and/or has a prominent spine. The bone is often misrepresented as a leafy bough.

The Bestiary tells us that Hyenas feed only on corpses; that they have a rigid spine and that their call can mimic the human voice. Certainly it

283. Alne. N.Yorks.
A Hyena bites a bone.

284. Carlisle. Cumb.
A Hyena with a rigid spine devours a corpse.

was thought until recently that the first item was true. The call does sound remarkably human. The carvers indicate a rigid spine by showing a very prominent backbone. In addition they said that it could change sex. (Modern zoologists say that the male and female genitalia are remarkably similar.) To change sex was an example of the utmost perversion, inconstancy and double mindedness.

So the Hyena could and did symbolise the Jews[27] or any other socially unacceptable group of the time.

We find one eating a floriated bone at Alne. The label above says Hyena. (This is a direct copy of a Bestiary picture.) There is one eating a corpse at Bradbourne and also at Carlisle, and swallowing a head at Burton Dassett. The strange beast at Swavesey could as easily be a Wolf as a Hyena. Wolves usually lick a paw in carvings so I suspect that this is a Hyena. Even the animal eating foliage at Alton is a Hyena, like at Alne. The Bestiary story concludes by saying that everyone who serves riches and an easy life is like this animal. They should have strength of purpose like a man instead of being weak and vacillating like a woman, and points out that 'Ye cannot serve God and Mammon.' Matt.6:24

[27]. Ref 33. p145.

285. Bradbourne. Derbys.
A Hyena attacks a body.

286. Swavesey. Camb.
Probably a Hyena with a stiff back.

Illust. 8.
A Hyena devours a corpse

145

287. Ilam. Derbys.
Probably a Hyena gorging on heads.
Possibly a 'Disgorging Monster' c.f. p.154.

All are examples of the perverted, the inconstant and the followers of an easy life.

288. Alton. Hants.
A Hyena with a 'floriated' bone.

289. Burton Dassett. Warw.
A Hyena goes off with a skull.

IBEX

Ibex for the Bestiary illustrator and carver are like mountain goats but with prominent straight horns.

The Bestiary story about the Ibex is short and to the point. This animal has two very strong horns, so strong that, if it falls from a high mountain they will bear the

290. Kings Lynn. Norf.
An Ibex secure in his knowledge of the Old and New Testaments.

291. Tewkesbury. Gloucs.
An Ibex falls headlong but 'no problem' he will be saved by his knowledge.

weight of the body and so it will be unharmed. The moral being that these are learned individuals who understand the Old and New Testaments. If anything happens to them they are supported 'as if on two horns' by all the good they have derived from the Old Testament and the Gospels.

At Burwell Ibex confront a cat representing Heresy. At Tewkesbury it is falling headlong and at Kings Lynn proud in the security of its knowledge.

292. Burwell. Camb.
Two Ibex engage the Cat of heresy.

IBIS

We recognise Ibis by their actions rather than by any close resemblance to our ideas about this wading bird. Some very obvious Spoonbills, as well as true Ibis, were the Bestiary illustrator's picture in the Ibis chapter. Unfortunately there is no chapter about the Spoonbill. So for the spiritual story we must refer to the Ibis.

The Bestiary begins by saying that the Ibis cleans out its bowels with its beak. (see picture from Lacock Abbey.) It continues by telling us that Ibis feed at the water's edge because they are

293. Lavenham. Suff.

A pair of Ibis investigate human carrion at the water's edge. The spoonbill was a frequent mistake made by the artists.

afraid to enter water, not knowing how to swim. They spend the day looking for dead fish or other bodies thrown on the shore.

This, they say, is an image of the carnally minded individual. Such a person 'feeds their soul on evil deeds and dares not leave the shores of a sinful life for the deeper waters of the mysteries of God.' It continues, 'if birds do not stretch out their wings they could not fly. So we, if we do not spread the wings of twofold love, cannot win through the storms of this world to the safe haven of the heavenly home.'

(Biologically Spoonbills, like the one we see at Stogursey, Fig.296, are filter feeders so cannot take eels but do feed at the water's edge. Ibis are not filter feeders nor do they stick to the water's edge and they might take a small eel.)

294. Lacock Abbey. Wilts.

An Ibis cleans out his back passage with his beak.

295. Kilpeck. H&W.
An Ibis attends to carrion instead of braving the open sea for more wholesome food.

296. Stogursey. Som.
An Ibis in spoonbill disguise feeds on evil deeds.

LAMIA

Lamiae appear in the Bible but only in the Latin Vulgate version. In Isaiah 34:14 and 13:21 it is a beast dwelling in cities already destroyed and laid waste. The AV translates the same word as screech owl.

The Lamia of folklore is a female monster and I have two possible examples. She can take whatever shape she wishes and seduces young men for a pastime and, as if that were not enough, she also enjoys killing children.

Both examples might be Harpies and the one at Cheriton Bishop is so described; however their overt sexuality suggests to me

297. West Bagborough. Som.
Lamia, eater of children.

that they might be Lamiae. There is an illustration in a book by Heinz Mode[28] that exactly fits the Cheriton Bishop version of the Lamia.

[28]. Ref 46.

298. Cheriton Bishop. Devon.
Lamia, seducer of young men.

LEUCROTA

This was a very swift animal that was said to live in 'India', had cloven hooves, a horse's head, haunches of a stag and a mouth that opened as far as the ears. Instead of a set of teeth it had one continuous bone and its voice was not unlike that of people talking. Some Bestiaries acknowledge that a relationship between a Lion and a Hyena produces the Leucrota. This is an adulterous union similar to the Lion with the Pard who produce the sterile Leopard.[29]

There seem to be no moral stories attached to it. I offer this strange animal from Earl Soham as a possible candidate. The tail is like that of one in a 12th Century Bestiary[30] and several others. The jaw is certainly emphasised and relatively toothless.

[29]. Ref 33 p147.

[30]. Ref 58.

299. Earl Soham. Suff.
Possibly a Leucrota; offspring of adultery between a lion and a hyena; therefore a crossbreed and sterile.

Illust. 9.
Leucrota Ref.58.

LEVIATHAN

The huge sea creature, the Leviathan, had his home in the great deep.

'The earth is full of thy riches, so is this great and wide sea, wherein are things creeping innumerable, both small and great beasts. There go the ships, there is that Leviathan whom thou hast made to play therein.' Ps.104:25-26.

A whale or great fish swallows Jonah. (see Whale and Dolphin.) There is often some confusion between this whale and Leviathan in ancient writings. As Christ tells us in Matt 12:40. 'For as Jonah was three days and three nights in the whale's belly; so shall the Son of Man be three days and three nights in the heart of the earth.' As such the whale's jaws symbolised the gates of Hell from which

300. Lincoln Cathedral.
Judgement porch. The mouth of Leviathan with attendant devils and perishing sinners.

Christ escaped on the third day. So in at least this respect the 'whale' was the same as Leviathan whose jaws symbolised the gates of Hell. In Job Ch 41. there is the following description of Leviathan that I have shortened to highlight those aspects that the Medieval artist loved to portray. 'Canst thou draw out Leviathan with a hook; his scales are his pride; out of his mouth go burning lamps and sparks of fire leap out. His breath kindleth coals and a flame goes out of his mouth. The sword of him that layeth at him cannot hold. He esteemeth iron as straw

301. Conques. Aveyron.
'Ushered into the jaws of death and doors of Hell.'

and brass as rotten wood. He maketh the sea to boil like a pot. He is a king over the children of pride.'

Sinners disappear into the mouth of Leviathan, chained and prodded by demons in many a Doom picture as at Conques. France. The same picture appears on the right side of the few remaining Doom paintings that still exist in England.

There is a passage in Rev. 20:12-13; which could relate to the Leviathan. 'when the books were opened and the dead were judged out of the things which are written in the books...and the sea gave up the dead which were in it; and death and hell delivered up the dead which were in them'.

It does not mention him by name, but there is good authority for the type of picture[31] where a 'Great Beast' personifies the sea that gives up its dead at the end of Time. The beast that to us looks like a

302. Bourges. Cher.
A fiery and disgusting end.

303. Horning. Norf.
One devil has his way; another is tamed in the stocks.

crocodile at Rollright (Fig.304) is probably just such a personification, or Leviathan himself, here shown bringing up a head. He is not swallowing it as one might have assumed. This is all occurring in a heavenly milieu with a sun disc for God above and stars all around.[32]   There is an analogous animal spewing out a head on the font at Tissington. (Fig.305) All the other figures on the same font associate with the triumph of Christ. There is an Agnus Dei, a bird for the Holy Spirit, a Crocodile and Hydrus and possibly Adam and Eve. So it would be reasonable to guess that this large jawed beast with a long coiled up tail is a Leviathan of the same sort as the one at Rollright. (Note 4.) (Generally known as 'Disgorging monsters.')

[31]. Ref 52. p178

[32]. R.W. of 62. Personal comm.

DISGORGING MONSTER VARIANTS

304. Gt. Rollright. Oxon.
One man still in his shroud, another delivered up from death and Hell.

305. Tissington. Derbys.
A sea monster delivers up the dead at the end of time.

306. Echillais. Charente Maritime.
A disgorger not a devourer.

307. Adel. W. Yorks.
A husband and wife pair and a fish (Christian) disgorged at the time of the Resurrection of the dead. The Hare too, is safe in the rock of Christ.

308. Gt. Durnford. Wilts. Font.
Pillars of the Church disgorged by a circuit of heads.

309. Elkstone. Gloucs.
Keystone in the half dome of the apse. A central belt and knot for strength and eternity. Four creating and guarding heads. Compare with Fig.325.

LINDWORM

The name Lindworm describes wingless and legless dragons that emerge from the ground. They feature more in old folk memory than in Bestiary lore and are held to symbolise the dangers and temptations hidden about our way.

310. N. Cadbury. Som.
Lindworms rise from the ground to plague us.

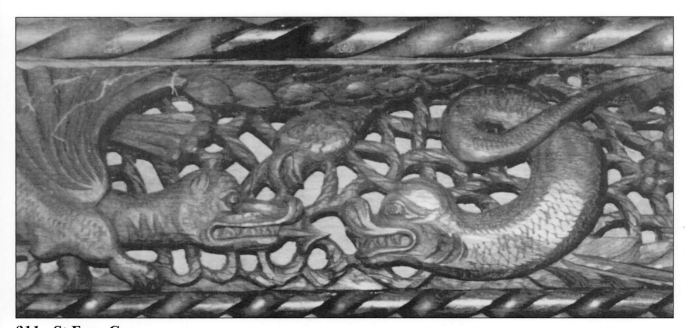

311. St Ewe. Corn.
A wingless flightless dragon fights a Wyvern.

LION

The Lion is the King of Beasts. We feel an instinctive agreement with this statement possibly because we inherit the symbol from six thousand years of Middle Eastern and European civilisations. It can symbolise Christ, and on occasions even God; but, like so many beasts, it can sometimes symbolise the opposite, the Devil.

'The Devil walketh about as a roaring Lion seeking whom he may devour.' 1 Pet.5:8. This verse is the source for all the negative qualities

312. Exeter Cathedral. Courtenay tomb.
A Lion keeps watch for the second coming.

313. Broadclyst. Devon.
A Lion on guard and watchful.

that we may encounter in Lion carvings.

The Bestiary gives a long list of characteristics to the Lion of which four are important.

Lions sleep with their eyes open: which, the Bestiary says, is like our Lord who fell asleep in the body on the Cross, and was buried; all the while his Godhead kept watch. It quotes Ps 121:4. 'He that keepeth Israel shall neither slumber nor sleep.' So the Lion can be on guard even though 'asleep.' He guards against sin and devils and is alert for the dreadful Day of Judgement. This is his function on a tomb when placed at the foot of the valiant knight or when he is part of a funerary monument. Just occasionally we see him with just one eye open giving an even better impression of relaxed awareness.

Lions when hunted would cover their tracks to avoid pursuit. Artists and carvers give the Lion a very bushy tail to illustrate this point. Christ, when he entered the womb of the Virgin Mary, left no trace. The Lion with a bushy tail is therefore a reminder of the Incarnation. Other writers say that the bushy

314. Eardisley. H&W.
A watchful Lion with maybe one eye closed.

tail shows that Christ concealed His deity whilst walking amongst mankind. They also say that the tail raised over the Lion's back signifies 'Justice that is placed over us' and therefore a reminder of the Judgement to come.

Lions are born dead. Three days later the parents restore the cubs to life by roaring and by licking them. The parallel is with God the Father who brings His Son to life at the Resurrection and, by extension, our New Birth after Baptism or conversion. (Note 5.)

Human Beings do not enrage him so long as they do not harm him. This is an example to all unreasonable people.

He is afraid of a white cock. He spares prisoners and those lying on the ground. He will eat an ape when ill.

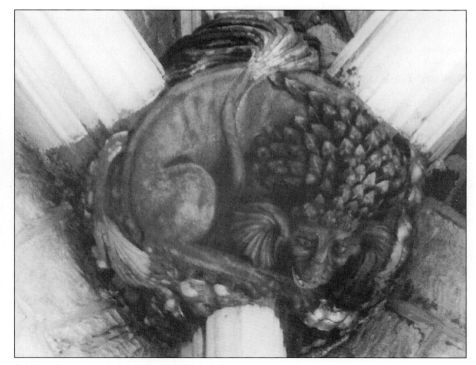

315. Exeter Cathedral. Roof boss.
The Lion roars to bring new-born to life.

The Lion appears in many stories in the Bible. There are numerous pictures of Samson, Judg.14.6. and David 2 Sam 23:20 rending Lion's jaws. (Fig.277 and 316. I like the tongue between the teeth to indicate the enormous effort being used.) These are bad Lions being destroyed and the metaphor reminds us of Christ destroying the gates of Hell, thereby delivering us from the power of Satan.

A Lion is the symbol of St. Mark. St Mark's gospel begins with the voice of one crying in the wilderness; this is St John the Baptist. Because the Lion comes from the wilderness the early Church chose it from the animals in Ezekiel's vision Ezek 10:14 and in the Revelation 4:7, to be the symbol of St. Mark.

316. Lincoln Cathedral.
Samson rends the Lion's jaws; tongue between teeth with the effort involved.

Daniel in the Lion's den, another 'favourite story', is a fruitful source of very many lion carvings: more so on the continent than in England. The picture is usually that of a pair of Lions, or Lion heads, either side of a man. It just so happens that a man holding a Lion in either hand is a picture inherited from Assyria. The Assyrians

317. Norwich Cathedral.
The Lion of St Mark.

318. Widecombe. Devon.
The Lion of Judah.

perfected the style several thousand years earlier. Some 'Daniel in the Lion's den' carvings are highly stylised derivatives of this theme; borrowed by the carvers for this new purpose. The early Church had a prayer where the priest beseeches God to 'Deliver His servants as He delivered Isaac from the sacrifice, Daniel from the Lion's Den, and the children of Israel from the fiery furnace'.[33] So the story of Daniel

319. La Sauve Majeur. Gironde.
Daniel quite safe in the Lion's den. c.f. Fig.274.

carries several shades of meaning. Daniel is a 'Type' of Christ and the Resurrection; and encourages the anxious believer to trust in deliverance. Fig.274, 319.

Leo is a sign of the Zodiac and like all such signs may be comparing and contrasting Heaven with humble earth.

Christ is the Lion of Judah who opens the Seven Seals and presides over all that happens at the end of Time. Rev 5:5.

Good Lions fight Evil Dragons in many carvings everywhere and always appear to be winning. This makes a lovely metaphor for the spiritual battle.

[33]. Ref 3. p73.

320. Gloucester Cathedral.
The battle between good and evil.

321. Avington. Berks.
A Lion in a church dedicated to St Mark.

322. Melbury Bubb. Dorset.
The Lioness gives birth through her mouth.
c.f. Note 5. p.265

323. Romsey Abbey. Hants.
The Lion of Justice and New Life.

LIZARD

Lizards shared with snakes the same general aura of evil although some of them had their own special redeeming features. The Bestiary classes together Lizards, Salamanders, Newts and Frogs. Lizards and snakes both had the capacity to crawl through a crack between some stones in order to slough off the old skin, then to reappear apparently rejuvenated, on the other side. The Bestiary gives this story a positive application. 'We must put off the old Adam for Christ's sake and seek Christ the spiritual rock, the straight gate.' Preachers sometimes gave this story an opposite interpretation especially with regard to snakes or serpents. They said that this was an example of the Devil's apparently

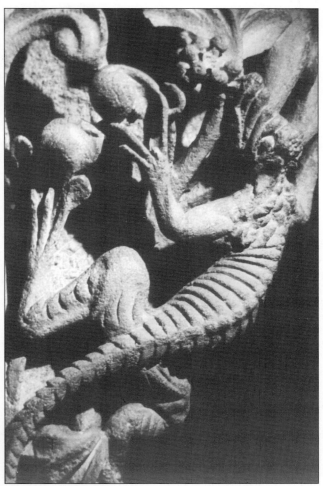

324. Wells Cathedral.
The Lizard seeks renewal from the grapes/wine/blood of Christ.

325. Iffley. Oxon.
A Lizard bites its tail in a symbolic form of rejuvenation. Streams of living water flow from almost feline heads. Pine cones represent the resurrection and a life after death. c.f. Fig. 76, 309.

endless capacity for rejuvenation and shows his deepest perfidy.

Besides sloughing off the old skin when it was old, the Lizard would also seek the rising sun through an east facing chink, there to renew its eyesight. There may be an allusion to this in the little head that looks out of the stone of an east facing arch at Barfrestone; (Fig. 327) a man seeking renewal in Christ (the sun.)

163

At Iffley a Lizard appears to bite its own tail in a symbolic form of rejuvenation. It has around it pine cones for eternity and four faces from which streams of living water flow. (Birds and other winged animals, biting or preening their wing feathers are another common metaphor for restoration and renewal.) There is a famous Lizard at Wells where it seems to be feeding on fruit, (seeking Christ) in much the same way as the bird does in the vine. There is an evil Lizard at Ashcombe amongst some frogs and snakes.

326. Ashcombe. Devon.
A Lizard shares a pew end with other reptiles, snakes and frogs.

327. Barfrestone. Kent.
A face seeking the Lord at the most easterly point like a Lizard would seek the morning sun.

164

LOCUST

328. Exeter Cathedral.
The Locust of the Apocalypse.

In no way to be confused with the everyday plague Locust, there is one special Biblical Locust in Rev. 9:7-10. 'And the shapes of Locusts were like unto horses prepared unto battle, and on their heads were as it were crowns of gold, and their faces were as the faces of men...and they had tails like unto scorpions, and there were stings in their tails; and their power was to hurt men five months.' They would have power over those of mankind who did not have the seal of God upon their foreheads.

There are two interpretations for the carving at Exeter. It is either a Revelation Locust or Aristotle in the story of Aristotle and Campaspe. Campaspe was a lady of uncertain reputation who made even wise Aristotle fall for her. She made him carry her round the garden on all fours, as if he were a horse. There are other pictures of this story in France. The moral being that even wisdom is no defence against the wiles of women. However at Exeter the animal has a head in the tail, like an evil Amphisbaena, and wears a crown as in the Biblical story. Aristotle might have been naively unwise but was not evil, which is the intention here. So I prefer the Locust description that fits the figure very well.

MANTICHORE

This is a wonderful name, probably derived from the Persian for man eating tiger, but given a much more fanciful description by the Bestiary. The Mantichore was very fierce; with a triple row of teeth set in a man's face on a lion's body. It was so strong it could jump any ditch and it delighted in eating human flesh. It had the voice of a Sibyl by which it could seduce individuals from the

329. Kilpeck. H&W.
The Mantichore, evil in all his ways.

paths of virtue and proclaim unwholesome doctrines in opposition to the sound doctrine of the Apostles. (The triple row of teeth defeats every illustrator and carver.)

It is yet another disguise for the Evil One.

Curiously the Mantichore is also an attribute of Jeremiah, presumably because he foretold the destruction (eating) of Jerusalem by Nebuchadnezzar in 586 BC.

330. Bristol. St Mary Redcliffe. N. Porch.
A Mantichore.

331. Barfrestone. Kent.
A Mantichore.

332. Denston. Suff.
A Mantichore.

333. North Cerney. Wilts.
A Mantichore on an outside wall.

MOLE

Moles are rare in church carvings. There is one at Kilham, Yorks. It faces towards someone being baptised in a tub font in the next roundel;[34] A Mole appears to be blind and therefore must live in perpetual darkness. An excellent example of those absorbed in earthly cares or vain delights and a symbol of the heretic or those blind to the Faith. However we can obtain enlightenment and True Faith through the rites of Holy Church; the message of these two little roundels.

334. Kilham. ER.Yorks.
A Mole comes out of the darkness to enlightenment via baptism.

[34]. Ref R.W. of 62. Personal comm.

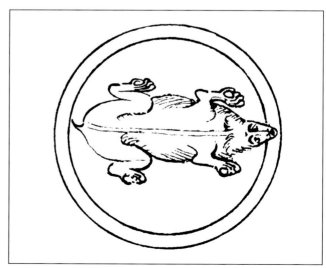

Illust. 10.
A Mole.

THE MONSTROUS RACES

We are all aware that people in the Middle Ages believed in the existence of individuals who had both human and animal characteristics. The Antipodes are a well-known name for such a tribe. Their feet faced the wrong way. Very few people had actually seen any of them but those who said that they had were of such unimpeachable authority that the doubters were silenced. They existed, so they must be in the Plan for God's world. On the Mappa Mundi at Hereford they occupy places on the circumference of the

335. Stone. Bucks.
A Pygmy on his cabbage leaf takes on a Goliath-Dragon.

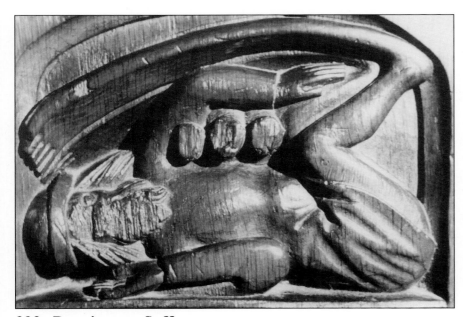

336. Dennington. Suff.
A Sciapod sheltering from the desert sun.

known world. They are farthest from the centre that is Jerusalem, the Heavenly City. Theologians raised the question; 'Do they have souls?' 'Are they degenerate human forms or are they false animals?' They came to the conclusion that they did indeed have souls. People with souls need to be saved and it is the Church's duty to find them and preach the Gospel to them. This is why we find examples of monstrous races in our churches. They are an

169

expression of the ultimate in the range of missionary activity. There is an excellent large book that describes the evolution of their curious story.[35] This is not the place for that story but the following is a list of those we may find in our churches.

Blemyae.

They have their faces in their chests.

Sciapod.

He has one giant foot on which he can hop at great speed and under which can hide from the sun.

Cynocephali.

These are dog headed people who bark instead of using human speech.

Callitrix.

They have very long hair.

Cyclops.

They have only one eye.

Panotii.

They have very large ears.

Hippopodes

They have horses' feet.

Four Eyes.

They have four eyes and come from 'Ethiopia.'

PYGMIES.

These short people are not the Pygmies of West Africa. They almost certainly represent

337. Souvigny. Allier.
Cyclops.

varieties of Dwarf. Ancient Greco-Roman writers say that they had an annual battle with the Cranes but do not say why. The 'boy' riding a Crane at Lincoln is therefore probably a Pygmy. Fig.102 Ancient writers said that three, or even seven, could stand under a cabbage leaf. This may explain the little figure on the font at Stone, Bucks. He is standing on a cabbage leaf. M.D.Anderson says on other grounds that she thinks it is a Pygmy. She adds that such a Pygmy represents David here fighting a Dragon /Goliath.

The experts of the Middle Ages thought that Pygmies represented a stage in Man's development. They believed that the embryo started as a sperm, became a shapeless form, then an Ape shape, then a Pygmy shape and finally a man.

338. Adderbury. Oxon.
Cyclops.

There are many other races of whom we may have heard but who rarely feature in carvings. They include: <u>Amazons;</u> women with only one breast . <u>Androgyna;</u> are half men and half women. <u>Anthropophagi;</u> are man eaters. <u>Troglodytes;</u> live in caves.

All these creatures were objects of fascination. They lived 'beyond the pale' and were a challenge for missionary activity.

[35] . Ref 31.

339. Ripon. N.Yorks.
Blemya with his head in his chest.

340. Ufford. Suff.
A long haired Callitrix.

341. Ufford. Suff.
One of the dog headed Cynocephali.

342. Vezelay. Yonne.
Cynocephali.

343. Vezelay. Yonne.
Panotii with very large ears.

344. Souvigny. Allier.
Hippopodes or Horse footed.

345. Souvigny. Allier.
Four eyes, the Ethiopian.

MOUSE AND RAT and also see Cat

Mice feature rarely in our carvings but are easy to recognise. They join together to hang the cat at Malvern. Fig.75 Fearsome cats catch Mice on fonts at Hodnet Fig.74 and Kirkburn. In these two carvings the poor Mice are souls in the grip of the Devil.

That Mice were extraordinarily fertile was common knowledge, hence by implication they were regarded as particularly lascivious. From this observation it followed that, as in the common parlance of the

346. Meavy. Devon. Roof boss.
Possibly St Colman who was kept awake when working in the scriptorium by a mouse nibbling his ear.

349. Kirkburn. ER.Yorks.
A devilish cat pounces on a defenceless mouse.

time, mousetrap could be synonymous with vulva.[36] The cat playing with a Mouse and sitting on a mousetrap as at N. Cadbury may be warning against who knows what sort of devilry.

The Mouse in the ear of the 'saint' at Meavy is a puzzle. It may refer to St Colman (of Kilmacduagh) who had a Mouse to nibble his ear to keep him awake in the scriptorium. He also had a fly to keep the place on the page when

173

he left for Divine service.

The Bestiary says that Mice represent greedy individuals who seek earthly goods and make the goods of others their prey. The Mice, to whom a Cat is playing the fiddle, may be wealthy citizens tempted by the Cat = Devil to go too far in their search for riches. Fig.79.

The rats of Heresy gnaw at the Christian World in the picture from Champeaux, Seine et Marne, France.

Some modern woodwork carries a tiny mouse somewhere on the surface. This is a signature of the carver and of no moral significance.

36. Ref 53.

348. North Cadbury. Som.
A cat sits on a mousetrap and plays with a mouse.

349. Champeaux. Seine et Marne
The Rats of heresy gnaw at the Christian world.

174

MULE and a little about Breeding and Muzzling

They are not easy to recognise and I offer only one possible candidate.

Ps 32:9 'Be ye not as the Mule which hath no understanding; whose mouth must be held in with bridle and bit, lest they come near unto thee.' The Bestiary writer says that the Mule represents those who follow foolish ways and points out that the Psalmist is warning men against being taken in by the wiles of the Devil. The writer also points out that the jaws of the disobedient should be restrained, so that compelled by fasting, they will yield to the rule of their Creator.

Other **muzzled** animals include Bears and, on earlier Norman carving, rather non specific beasts. In a church context these refer to sin now under control. We can imagine 'The wiles of the Devil' feeling like a burden of vice. The Mule, because it is a beast of burden could all too easily take on such a load. So the loaded Mule becomes a picture of a person weighed down by vice. Considering how common Mules must have been, one can only explain their rarity in carving by their rather feeble story line.

The chapter on the Mule in the Bestiary also contains a little homily on **breeding.** It says that human beings have produced this new species in an unnatural fashion by putting together asses and mares. Jacob tried to obtain a similar result by placing white stakes in front of his sheep when they were mating with the rams. He obtained a speckled flock. (see

350. Earl Soham. Suff.
A Mule; a picture of a man loaded down with sin.

351. Barfrestone. Kent.

An animal, possibly a bear, muzzled to show that desires are now under control.

Gen. 31.) It states further that the same process will happen with mares who should be in a position to see noble stallions as they conceive. Pigeon fanciers can try to influence the outcome by placing the image of a beautiful pigeon in the breeding loft. For the same reason it adds, pregnant women should not look at ugly beasts such as apes and monkeys, in case they should bring children into this world who resemble these creatures. 'For women's nature is such that they produce offspring according to the image they see or have in mind at the moment of ecstasy as they conceive.'

There are taboos about some things being 'not nice' enough for women to see, whereas for men there is no such restriction. This story would have been a strong reinforcer for such a 'superstitious' belief. A view that is still with us today.

NEBUCHADNEZZAR

Nebuchadnezzar was not an animal although he was compelled to behave like one and this carving might be difficult to place if we did not know his story. He was condemned 'to dwell with the beasts of the field, eat grass as oxen, and be wet with the dew of heaven.' Dan 4:25. This was the penalty foreshadowed in a dream that Daniel interpreted. He told Nebuchadnezzar that he must mend his ways and show mercy to the poor or else the above fate would befall him. For a year Nebuchadnezzar did nothing, and then at the height of his pride in the Babylon he had built, a voice came from heaven saying 'Thy kingdom is departed from thee.' He crawled around for seven years 'till his hairs

352. Feltwell. Norf.
Nebuchadnezzar 'eats grass as oxen.'

were grown like eagle's feathers, and his nails like bird's claws.' Ultimately his sanity returned, his understanding returned, and he blessed the Most High.

A terrible story of the sin of pride and how true it is that pride goes before a fall.

I apologise for this decapitated figure; it should have a face with a full beard. There are more presentable Victorian copies around but I have no photos. The figure from the chancel arch at Adel could also be Nebuchadnezzar. It bears more resemblance to him than it does to a Mantichore, which is the only other likely candidate for such a 'person.'

355. Adel. W.Yorks.
Chancel arch. Possibly Nebuchadnezzar in the grip of the devil.

OSTRICH

We recognise the Ostrich in carvings when we see a bird holding an iron horseshoe. We do have to know the Bestiary story about the Ostrich to appreciate the little moral that the picture is trying to tell us.

The Bestiary points out that the Ostrich has the feet of a camel, a cast iron digestion and lays its eggs at the rising of the constellation Virgilia (Pleiades). It covers the eggs with sand then goes off to follow these stars. This is not an example of bad parenting. It is quite the opposite. This is an example of the blessedness of leaving earthly ties and seeking those things that are above.

Other medieval commentators made parallels between the Ostrich and the Synagogue. This bird has wings (the Law) which cannot raise it to heaven. The Jews too have the Law but it cannot bring them salvation. A similar analogy condemns the Ostrich as an example of stupidity and hypocrisy for it had both wings yet could not fly and eggs that it did not hatch.

Ostriches are famous for their iron digestion; indeed their gizzards may be full of all sorts of metal items if they have the chance to find them. We also 'know' that Ostriches bury their heads in the sand. I have not been able to find a Bestiary reference but I suspect the notion was always around, and accounts for the carving of a bird with buried head at Eynesbury. (The idea is quoted as being in common parlance by 1563; O.E.D.)

In summary then an Ostrich is an encouragement to seek 'higher things'. It may, in some contexts, be a warning not to be foolish, not to be hypocritical and not to rely on the Old Law.

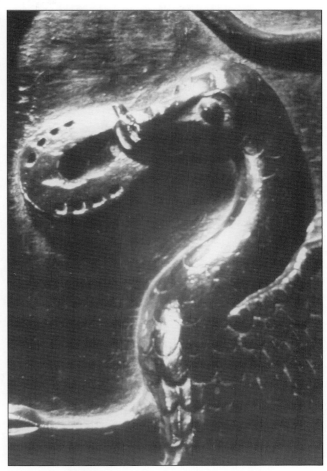

354. Stratford on Avon. Warw.
An Ostrich with his dose of iron.

355. Worcester Cathedral.
Ostriches with their horseshoes either side of a central Rogationtide figure.

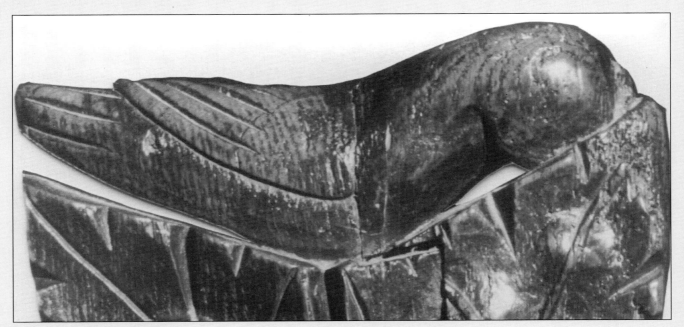

356. Eynesbury. Beds.
An Ostrich, head in sand.

OWL

Owls are always easy to recognise.

We can scarcely talk about Owls without adding the cliché...wise and old ... to the general discussion. This is a great pity since the concept was totally foreign to the people who did the medieval carvings. I think it is probably safe to say that Owls in Medieval churches are never 'wise old Owls'. For the record the wise old Owl story comes from Greek mythology where Minerva, the Goddess of Wisdom, had an Owl as her attribute and companion. It was not until the Renaissance that this concept became the common idiom.

The Bestiary talks of two sorts of Owls,

357. Norwich. Cathedral.
A sinner bears the reproofs of good people. Also often interpreted as a Jew ignoring the Good News borne by those all about him.

358. Wakefield. W.Yorks.
A creature that prefers the darkness.

Bubo and Noctua, but their symbolism is broadly the same. Owls prefer darkness to light and hence Owls came to symbolise the Jews who preferred the darkness of their ignorance under the Old Law, to the light of day in Christendom. There are many pictures of Owls being mocked by small birds. This is an example of the Sinner, who when his sins have come to light, has to bear the reproofs of good people. In a more general sense we find Owls as the symbol of darkness, and therefore Death. We often find them accompanying or foretelling death and disaster scenes.

Some Owls are a rebus, a sort of pictorial puzzle. Bishop Oldham (Owl-d-am) at Exeter has a whole chapel profusely decorated with Owls that preserve his name in perpetuity but without any moral connotation.

359. Gt. Malvern. H&W.
Mice hang the cat. (? Richard III.). The Owls as Tricoteuse watch.

360. Exeter Cathedral.
Bishop Oldham's = Owl-d-ham's chantry. A rebus.

361. Rimpton. Som.
An Owl amongst ivy.

Ox

We might mistake an Ox for the Bull of St Luke but the latter usually has wings.

The Ox like the Bull was a symbol of sacrifice. It was also a symbol of all those ordinary folk who patiently bore the yoke and labour to further the Kingdom of God. Traditionally it has the qualities of industry, patience and strength that are so necessary for real work. In the early Church it could be a symbol of Christ as the true sacrifice; or because 'with the plough of his cross he has turned the earth of our flesh.' It is also a symbol of the Prophets and Saints who worked so hard for the Faith.

A team of Oxen must have been a very common sight and maybe the team at Kingston St. Mary and the lonely one at Bishops Lydeard are just, like harvest festival, a present to the Lord of daily matters. However the Bestiary points out that oxen are symbols of preachers who successfully plough the soil of human hearts to prepare them to receive the heavenly seed of the Word.

Oxen, unless they relate to St Luke, are relatively rare in carvings in England but there is a famous font at St. Barthélemy, Liège where twelve front halves of Oxen support a font. This relates back to the furnishing of King Solomon's temple where in I Kings 7:25 a molten sea stands upon twelve Oxen. There are six Oxen placed near the top of Laon cathedral in honour it is said, of the Oxen that hauled the carts full of stone for the building. I have no photographs. Single heads of Oxen appear on many capitals and corbels of Romanesque churches in central and south west France. Here they seem to be a metaphor for Christ.

362. Kingston St Mary. Som.
Ploughing the souls of human hearts ?

The Ox and Ass that gaze on the infant Jesus in the crib do not appear in the New Testament story. There is a verse in Isaiah 1:3 that does give some authority for their appearance because it says; 'The ox knoweth his owner, and the ass his master's crib, but Israel doth not know, my people doth not consider.'

181

363. Bishops Lydeard. Som.
An Ox prepared to take the load.

364. St Julien de Jonzy. Saône et Loir.
Christ the Ox ?

182

PANTHER

It is very difficult to recognise Panthers in carvings because they look so like Lions. We have to go back to the Bestiary story and see how the illustrators of the Bestiaries coped with the differences to have any hope of coming up with an answer. I do not promise that my examples are incontrovertibly correct. The crucial clue lies in the fact that the Panther has very sweet breath. The illustrators and therefore the carvers show this in two ways. There is either a cone of exhaled breath or a long multitailed tongue. There are examples of both. (See Fig.365 and 366,) Sometimes there is no breath visible but we know from pictures in the Bestiaries that the position shown is that of an illustration in the Bestiary. (See the example at Alne; Fig.367; and Peasmarsh 370) where the Panther faces the serpent who flees into the bowels of the earth.

365. Milborne Port.
A Trinity. A Lion (Rt.) the Father; a Panther (Lt) Christ and a trefoil tongue from the Lion, the Holy Spirit.

366. Everton. S.Yorks.
Another Trinity; this Panther has a bifid tongue.

The Panther is a metaphor for Christ. The big cats, Lions, Leopards, Tigers and Panthers that all look so alike in carvings have very different stories to tell. The most surprising is the Panther. The Bestiary tells us that it is a beautiful beast, brightly coloured and tame. It is purely good with no negative qualities. The story goes that after a full meal the Panther slept for three days and rested in his den. He descended to the underworld where he chained the great Dragon. On waking he let out a roar and his breath was now very sweet. All the animals gather from far and near to follow this sweet smell. The Dragon alone hid away deep in his lair. 'Thus the Lord Jesus Christ, like the Panther, descended from heaven and saved us from the power of the Devil.' The Bestiary expands the story over several pages but the nub of it is as above.

367. Alne. N.Yorks.
A Panther faces the serpent/dragon forcing it to flee.

The Panther was famous for its 'goodness' long before Christianity. We can see a female Panther unselfishly fighting to save her young from a Hippogryphon on a grave slab from Paestum, Italy circa 340 BC.

A Panther 'calls' all the animals in a carving on a boss at Tewkesbury. It is part of an animal Trinity on the tympanum at Milborne Port and probably too at Everton, Yorks; and possibly at Fritwell, Oxon. (Note 6.). There is a Panther facing a Dragon on the arch at Alne. This picture comes straight from a Bestiary. The lettering above says Pantera, which means Panther.

Illust. 11.
Animals follow the sweet breath of the Panther.

184

368. Paestum. Italy.

A female Panther fights a Hippogriffon. She is altruistically protecting her children through love.

369. Tewkesbury. Gloucs.

A Panther (Christ) has called all the animals (us).

370. Peasemarsh. Sussex.

The serpent or the bone are lost from this large carving of a Panther or Hyena. I think a Panther the most likely.

PARD AND LEOPARD

Leopards we know, Lions we know, but Pards; what are Pards?

Again we must forget all our knowledge of modern natural history. The Pard was a very swift and bloodthirsty animal rather like a Leopard. It had a beard and they often drew it with a protruding tongue to indicate fierceness. The Bestiary writers thought of it as the original from which the Leo-Pard was derived. The Leo-Pard was born of the adulterous union of the Lioness with the male Pard. The Leopard was therefore a degenerate and sterile form of animal analogous to a mule in its

371. Hodnet. Shrops.
A very fierce Pard.

372. Dunblane. Stirling.
A Leopard; because it was sterile like the mule it became an emblem of Abbots or Abbesses.

origins. In this sterile form it became a suitable emblem for Abbots and Abbesses. (Fig.372, from Dunblane where it might be an emblem for a local dignitary.)

Biblical references always give the Leopard an evil connotation. Rev.13:2. 'And the beast I saw was like unto a Leopard...' Jer.13:23. 'Can the Ethiopian change his skin or the Leopard his spots?'

Bible commentators saw the Leopard's spots as

186

meaning spotted with sin, as the Devil can be full of a diversity of sins or the sinner guilty of a variety of wrongdoings.

However in Isiah.11:6, we have the story of a transformation. 'The wolf shall dwell with the lamb, and the Leopard shall lie down with the kid; and the calf and the young lion and the fatling together, and a little child shall lead them'. We find the Leopard and the Kid beautifully carved, cuddling up to each other at Bakewell. The Leopard has a serpent's tail to indicate Evil, while the Kid has wings for 'Good'. This was the transformation that occurs when Christ arrives, and from then on, leads. Other versions appear in France and possibly also in England. (See also under Rabbit.) and (Note 11).

Baptism was one way of entry to the Church and a point at which metaphorically we lose our beast like nature. There is a fierce animal that attacks on one side of a font at St Stephen in Brannel, Cornwall; but then plays cheerfully on another side. It may be such a Leopard.

Fierce Lion-like animals with protruding tongues and head turned full face are more likely to be Pards or Leopards

373. Little Walsingham. Norf.
Bearded and with protruding tongue, a likely Pard.

than Lions or Panthers.

Shakespeare four hundred years ago knew about Pards. (As You Like It. Act 2.7.149) 'A soldier... bearded like the Pard... seeking the bubble reputation even in the cannon's mouth.' This is, for most of us, the only reference we might remember to a Pard. The bearded soldier gains a fierce reputation because he resembles the bearded Pard.

374. Bakewell. Derbys.
'The Leopard shall lie down with the Kid.'

375. St Stephen in Brannel. Corn.
A Leopard/Pard before conversion ?

376. St Stephen in Brannel. Corn.
Leopards/Pards rejoice in this New Life.

377. Wormleighton. Warw.
A Pard or a sexy Dog.

PARROT AND CROSSBILL

A bird with a large solid looking beak is likely to be a Parrot, but they also paint and carve many other Parrots in a more natural fashion. There is one certain carving of Crossbills at Wells though it is not obvious that this was the intention of the carver. I include them here for convenience. Parrots feature more often in medieval painting than in carvings. A pattern of green birds on a red ground could make a pleasing covering for wall or screen; a design more frequently found than any carving. The Bestiary gives us no symbolic meaning even though it does note; a very strong beak on

378. Stowlangtoft. Suff.
A Parrot. A diversion from the spiritual life ?

379. Exeter Cathedral.
One of a pair of Parrots.

which the Parrot could fall head first yet be unharmed; and the capacity to mimic the human voice.

They describe Parrots as the Jongleurs of the animal world. Jongleurs were no doubt welcomed by the populace for diversion and entertainment. Such activity would be less than welcome by the Church who saw it as taking men's minds and the Christian's attention away from the concerns of the spirit.

There are Parrots at Exeter; note the two forwards and two backward facing toes, which is correct for the species. There are Crossbills at Wells with three forwards facing toes, though whether this is by accident or design, is unknown. There was an irruption of Crossbills recorded by Matthew Paris in 1251. They are alleged to have robbed fruit trees very grievously and poisoned the remaining fruit. So these Crossbills may be telling us of the destruction of the spiritual life or, they may be good because they feed on pine cones an early symbol of rebirth. A pair of birds also feeding on pine cones appear at Hereford cathedral. They are not obviously Crossbills, so both carvings may refer to the soul seeking the food of immortality.

380. Wells. Cathedral.
A pair of Crossbills.

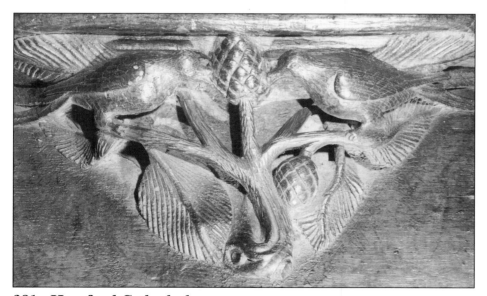

381. Hereford Cathedral.
A pair of birds feed on pine cones formerly a symbol of life after death.

PARTRIDGE

A rather nondescript bird apparently caring for an egg or two is likely to represent the Partridge.

The Bestiary writers surprisingly damn the Partridge on two counts. Firstly, they say it has homosexual tendencies. I do not know of a carving that demonstrates this. Secondly, it liked to steal eggs from a neighbouring Partridge, but this was of no avail, for when the chick hatches it hears the true mother's voice and quickly returns to her. This is the story alluded to in the carvings. The Bestiary uses a thought from Jerem.17:11. 'Like the Partridge that gathers a brood which she did not hatch, so is he who gets riches but not by right; in the midst of his days they will leave him, and at his end he will be a fool.'

382. Kirkburn. ER.Yorks.
Partridges stealing eggs; the chicks will hatch and return to their true parent.

The Partridge is the Devil who likes to rob the Creator of his offspring, but when they hear the voice of their true mother, Christ, they return. 'There is no miserable sinner who wishing to retract and repent cannot come to God. Holy Church will receive him.' In this way the Devil is denied a prize for his evil intentions.

So maybe this is why we may find them on an entrance arch to the church. The wanderer returns to mother Church. Likewise one appears on a font where we may start the Christian life. See the pictures from Kirkburn and Wold Newton.

Birds feeding on corn as at Acton, Suffolk though they may look like Partridges in the local cornfields, have only the general meaning of the Christian feeding on the bread of Christ. In the same way birds feeding on grapes are Christians in the branches of the 'True Vine.'

191

383. Wold Newton. ER.Yorks. Font.
A Partridge watches her egg.

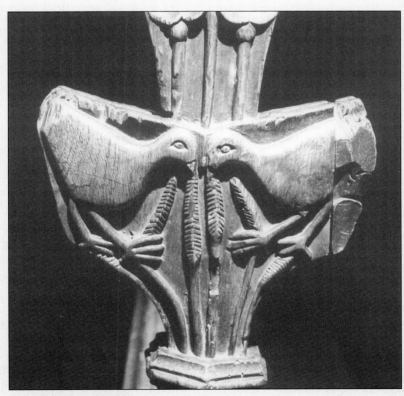

384. Acton. Suff.
Birds feed on the bread of life.

PEACOCK

The bird with the typical raised and beautiful tail that belongs to the male Peacock is easy to recognise. Less obvious is the bird who has bent down to peck at a foot and who often has a stumpy tail. This creature illustrates the Bestiary story about the Peacock.

The Peacock carries a variety of meanings.

Firstly, in Roman times it was a symbol of **immortality** used by the Emperors. The early Christians kept the same symbolism. In the Bestiaries there is a story about the flesh of the Peacock being so hard that even if buried for three days it does not putrefy. So it became a symbol of the **Resurrection.**

The Bestiary writers contrast the great beauty of the Peacock with the ugliness if its feet of which it was said to be greatly ashamed. They say that when praised and full of pride the Peacock's tail might rise and spread only to drop when it realised how ugly were its feet. In just such a way a man in the midst of success and splendour may suddenly become **ashamed of his sins.** So we have Peacocks biting their legs as at Bradbourne or pecking at hidden feet as at Bristol.

The Peacock has a most unpleasant and alarming cry that it sometimes utters by night. The Bestiary writers say that this is because of a sudden fear of losing its beauty. So too the Christian should be **afraid of falling from Grace.**

The eyes in the Peacock's tail were held to typify man's **foresight** that, when he fails to use it, results in a collapse similar to that of the laid low tail.

The Bestiary also adds that Solomon brought back a peacock from distant lands. 1 Kings 10:22. It signified the **Gentiles coming from the ends of the earth to Christ** who adorns them with the grace and splendour of many virtues. Such virtues are one of the additional benefits of Baptism as implied on the font at Hodnet. The Peacock there reminds us that Baptism gives us access to spiritual immortality.

385. Bristol Cathedral.

A normal Peacock on the Rt. and one ashamed of his feet on the Lt.

386. Hodnet. Shrops. Font.
A 'Gentile' comes to Christ to be adorned with many virtues

387. New Coll. Oxf.
A Peacock puffed up with pride.

388. Barwick. Devon.
A Peacock reproaches itself over its feet.

389. Bradbourne. Derbys.
A Peacock bites his foot in shame; as we should be ashamed of our sins.

194

PELICAN

It is surprising that we all know this bird as a Pelican when it bears so little resemblance to the real bird. We always find it, beak to breast, standing over a nest of chicks.

Except for the Eagle and the Lion, the Pelican is probably the most frequent and certainly one of the most potent of our animal symbols. The usual picture is of the 'Pelican in her Piety', and this is her story.

The Bestiary says that the Pelican shows exceeding love towards its young. The young as they grow become rebellious and strike their parents in the face. The parents strike back and kill them. After three days the Mother Pelican opens her breast so that her blood pours over the dead bodies that all come back to life. It is easy to see the parallel between this episode and with ourselves who

390. Salle Norf.
A Pelican revives her fledglings.

391. Brent Knoll. Som.
The Pelican forgives then resuscitates her children.

have despised and attacked God and therefore merited death. Christ on the Cross has His side pierced. The blood and water that flow out create the exact analogy for the healing actions of the Mother Pelican. We speak of the redeeming blood of Christ that pays for our sin so that we can come to life again. The Pelican has become a symbol of the Eucharist but we need to know the whole story to appreciate the force of the metaphor. It is not surprising that we find the Pelican in virtually every medieval church.

PHOENIX

The Phoenix rising from the ashes is a very obvious symbol of Christ's Death and Resurrection but is surprisingly uncommon in medieval church carvings. It is also not very easy to recognise but a bird associated in some way with flames should be a Phoenix.

There is only one Phoenix alive at any one time. At the end of five hundred years it builds a pyre of sweet herbs and burns there in the sun's rays. From the ashes comes a worm that turns into the

392. Garway. H&W.
A risen Phoenix with a tongue of the Holy Spirit.

393. Champeaux. Seine et Marne.
A Phoenix rises from the flames a picture of the Resurrection and preening, a picture of rejuvenation.

new Phoenix rising from the flames.

The Bestiary quotes from Jn.10:17,18. 'Therefore doth my Father love me because I lay down my life, that I may take it again. No man taketh it from me but I lay it down of myself. I have power to lay it down and I have power to take it again.'

(Earl Soham, this is the only explanation I can see for this figure.)

394. Earl Soham. Suff.
Possibly a Phoenix.

395. Kilpeck. H&W.
A Phoenix on a nest of flames.

PIG SOW SWINE and also see Boar

These are easy to recognise but it can be more difficult to ascribe a meaning to all of them.

The Bestiary gives us the story we should expect of the Pig, namely that it is a filthy beast, a lover of mud and slime. It says that Sows signify sinners, the unclean and heretics; and points out that they are like those who bewail their misdoing one minute and the next return to the mire. 2 Pet.2:22. 'The dog is returned to his vomit again; and the sow to her wallowing in the mire.'

A few of the carvings in our churches may present this thought to us, but I have no

396. Worcester Cathedral.
A Sow and piglets. This site is God's chosen place.

397. Ripon. N.Yorks.
A Sow plays to her piglets. One vice encouraging another.

certain example.

Some tell the very different and rather delightful story of *St. Brannock and the Sow.* Legend has it that when he was laying the foundations of his church, the work that had been done by day would be undone the same night. He dreams about a different site on which he should build the church. He would recognise this place by finding a Sow and her litter under an oak tree. It happens as foretold and he builds the church in no time at all. So the Sow with her litter, quite common in West Country churches, tells us that this is a Divinely Chosen Place.

198

Pigs playing the bagpipe, harp, and pipe are not unusual in carving. They represent the greedy, the lustful, the sensual and the thoughtless parodying the glories of Holy Church and epitomise the unholy behaviour of certain elements in society.

Christ's persecutors were the Jews. Jews may not eat pork. Thus, in a roundabout way, pigs may equate with Jews in some Romanesque sculpture.

There is a Pig or Swine on an early tympanum at Parwich that may represent the Gadarene Swine into which Christ cast the unclean spirits. Swine in such a context can

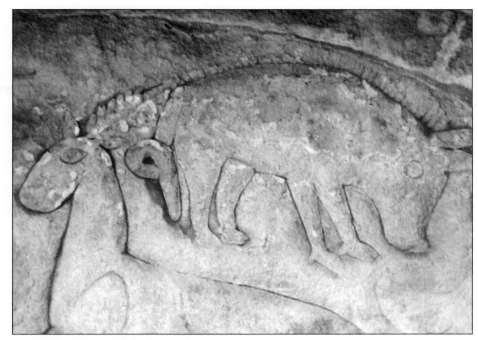

398. Parwich. Derbys. Tympanum.
Possibly one of the Gadarene swine.

represent madness. Madness was a subdivision of 'wrath' or 'anger' one of the Seven Deadly Sins.

For the Boar, the wild male member of the pig family, see its own chapter.

399. Over. Camb.
The Sow as the mount for a naked gluttony.

RABBIT   and also see Hare

Rabbits are difficult to distinguish from Hares in church carvings and for Rabbit read Hare for that is virtually certain to be the intended subject. Rabbits were not really established in Britain until the 13th Century. The three Rabbits sharing ears on many West Country roof bosses the so called 'Tinners' Rabbits'; probably have nothing to do with Tinners. See under Hare for suggestions as to their meaning.

The delightful dog and 'Rabbit' paired together at Kilpeck might be a poetic analogy for that passage in

400. North Bovey. Devon.
'Tinners Rabbits.'

401. Kilpeck. H&W. Apse, East end.
The hunter and the hunted lie down together.

Is.11:6. where all varieties of attacker and attacked come together and 'The Wolf shall dwell with the lamb, and the Leopard lie down with the kid.' (See under Pard and Leopard for another example.) The same analogy appears at Rodez where a dog and cat share a position of comfort together. Truly a time when all enmity is lost. (See Note 11 for another beautiful example of this Epiphany announcement.)

Rabbits like Hares are an attribute of Cowardice.

The animals carved disappearing into and looking out of burrows at Forrabury are probably the Hare and Conies mentioned in Prov.30:26 and Ps.104:18; where they seek refuge in the Rock of Christ. (But also see Fox, Goat and Hare.)

402. Forrabury.
Conies find shelter in the rock of Christ.

403. Rodez. Aveyron.
Cat and Dog, sworn enemies now at peace. c.f. Fig.533, 534.

RAVEN

There are very few Raven carvings and those that there are could carry either positive or negative meanings. We can recognise them as birds with large beaks involved in some fairly characteristic actions; such as pecking at the eyes or bringing food to their young or to a person. The other bird with a large beak is the Parrot but we rarely find it engaging in any obvious activity.

The Bestiary tells us that the Raven pecks out the eyes before attacking

404. Exeter Cathedral. Roof boss.
Penance and confession pluck out the eye of covetousness ?

405. Ely Cathedral.
A Raven attacks the eye of a sheep.

the rest of a corpse. It also says that the Raven will not feed its newly hatched young properly until they are covered in black feathers like the parent. It tells us that the Raven signifies the blackness of sinners. Prov.30:17. 'The eye that mocketh at his father and despiseth to obey his mother, the Ravens of the valley shall pick out.' Then the Bestiary goes on to say that the Raven signifies the Gentiles quoting Job 38:41 'Who provideth for the Raven his food? when his young ones cry unto God, they wander for lack of meat.' It points out that 'Food is given to the young ones of the Raven, the sons of the Gentiles, when they wish to be converted.' This and the statement about not feeding the young till they have their feathers (clothes) on, unlocks the meaning of the little label stop carving at St Decuman's, Watchet. The naked Gentile will be fed when he puts on the cloak provided by the Church.

At Southwell Raven parents obtain food for their young from the evergreen ivy growing out of the mouth of a Green Man, here representing Christ and the Church.

The Raven at Ely is on a misericord about Noah and the Flood. The Raven was the first bird to be sent out when the water subsided. It never returned; a fact held to confirm an essentially selfish and sinful

406. Southwell. Notts.
Ravens feed their young with food from the evergreen ivy, a symbol of eternal life issuing from the mouth of the Green Man (Christ).

nature.

The beautifully carved Raven at Exeter may be telling us a preacher's story about a sinner. The preacher would say that Penance and Confession are like Ravens for they pull out the eyes of Covetousness from the Soul that is dead in trespass and sin.[37]

[37]. Ref 49.

407. Watchet, St Decuman's. Som.
The naked gentile will be fed when clothed by the teaching of the Church.

RHINO

The only Rhinos I know are on the tower at Camerton church and on the west face of Laon Cathedral.

The Bestiary describes two animals that have one horn, the Monoceros and the Unicorn. It adds that the Monoceros is called Rhinoceros in Greek. Early writers knew the Rhino as an animal from the East that possessed a horn with aphrodisiac properties. These early writers had a clear mental image of the Rhino that was clearly separate from the Unicorn. The Bestiary descriptions of both Monoceros and Unicorn made them virtually indistinguishable. There was inevitable confusion when the people who had seen neither tried to illustrate the very similar descriptions. So for the meaning of Rhinos, see under Unicorn.

408. Camerton. Som.
A Rhino or Monoceros, the same name as has the Unicorn.

SALAMANDER

Salamanders are usually spotted with a forked or knotted tail. They may or may not have wings and can vary enormously in size. Truly giant ones occur in Cornwall.

The Salamander has two opposing characteristics that derive from the qualities the Bestiary gives it. The more familiar one that it can pass unharmed through fire comes from long before Christ's time. This great facility illustrates the bright future for the Christian who will be able to pass unscathed through the fires

409. Stone. Bucks. Font.
A knotted tail, one of the traits of the Salamander .

of temptation. It accounts for the frequent appearance of a Salamanders on fonts which are the symbolic entry point for the Christian life. A Biblical analogy occurs in Is.43:1-2. 'O Israel fear not, I have redeemed thee, I have called thee by name, thou art mine,...when thou walkest through fire, then shalt thou not be burned, neither shalt the flame kindle upon thee.' There are other Biblical analogies especially the three men who survive the fiery furnace, in Dan 3:21.

(In the Middle Ages asbestos was known as Salamander's wool.)

In the Bestiary there is the less well known idea of the Salamander being extremely poisonous; the most poisonous of all known animals. If it fell in a well, all who afterwards drank from there would die. If it climbed an apple tree all the fruit immediately became extremely poisonous. Where we see a Salamander that is not on a font then we are probably looking at one of the disguises of the Evil One. Such, I suspect are the figures at Swinbrook and probably at Bampton.

410. Swinbrook. Oxon.
A poisonous Salamander with a forked tail.

411. Luxulyan. Corn. Font.
After baptism we should be able to pass through the fires of temptation unscathed.

412. Tregony / St Cuby. Corn. Font.
A forked tail, another Salamander trait.

413. Bampton. Oxon.
A Salamander poisons the fruit tree.

SERRA

The Bestiaries feature some very beautiful pictures of this early notion of a *flying fish*, although the word means *sawfish* and refers to both species in the one chapter in the Bestiary. There are two different sets of pictures from which the carvers took their models. One set features a dorsal crest running the length of the body; the other a pair of wings.

The story of the winged Serra says that it loved to race ships and

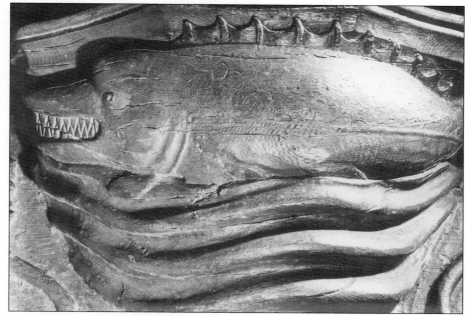

414. Bishop's Stortford. Herts.
A Serra as Sawfish, prepared to sink the ship of the faithful.

415. Eynesbury. Beds.
Probably a Serra or two; they start well but fail to fulfil their own expectations.

would do so for up to forty furlongs; after that distance it sank back exhausted into the depths. The Bestiary says that this is like those who at the beginning set their hand to good works but who are ultimately overwhelmed by all kinds of vices. The ship is the just man sailing serenely on through fair weather and foul. 'He that endureth to the end shall be saved.' Matt.10:22; is the accompanying Biblical thought.

According to other

authorities the Serra was evil and desired to sink the ship of the faithful. This it did with a sharp snout and a saw like crest that could pierce the underside of the hull. This gives us the fierce crested fish that we may confuse with a dolphin (but dolphins do not have a dorsal crest).[38]

There are examples at Bishop's Stortford, Lakenheath, Eynesbury and probably at Burford.

[38]. Ref 29.

416. Lakenheath. Suff.
A possible Serra falling into the waves.

417. Burford. Oxon.
An aggressive sawfish.

SERPENT

The snake is the one symbol for which there are so many shades of meaning, so many associations whether classical, subconscious, literary or Biblical, that it is impossible to say that a particular Serpent means just one thing. We have to juggle and hold in our mind several strands of thought that may contradict or complement each other at one and the same time. To summarise some of these associations and starting with the Bible...

418. East Meon. Hants. Font.
The Serpent beguiles Eve in the Garden of Eden.

The Devil as tempter. 'Now the Serpent was more subtle than any beast of the field...' Gen.3:1-6. The Temptation in the Garden of Eden is probably the one picture that comes to mind when we think about Snakes and the Bible. It occurs occasionally in carving on fonts as at East Meon. This association with Baptism has biblical authority; 1 Cor 15:22; 'For as in Adam all die, even so in Christ shall all be made alive.' and Gen 3:15. 'and I will put enmity between thee and the woman and between thy seed and her seed: it shall bruise thy head, and thou shalt bruise his heel.'

From the Bestiary we have three stories relating directly to the snake.

(One). When it grows old it renews itself by first fasting, then squeezing through a crack in a rock and sloughing off the old skin. 'We put off the Old Adam and through the strait gate seek Christ.' (Fig.325) The capacity for self renewal as in the Bestiary story becomes beneficent in the healing properties of the Caduceus, the

419. Hinton Parva or Little Hinton. Wilts. Font.
A Serpent that may have left its poison when it came to drink of the water of baptism.

209

emblem of the medical profession, where two serpents entwine. Preachers sometimes took an opposite point of view and saw this ability as an example of the Devil's perfidy in his being able to perpetuate himself apparently endlessly.

(Two). It leaves its poison behind in a pit when it goes to drink. 'So we, when we come to Church must leave behind earthly and evil desires.' I wonder if the knotted snake on the font at Little Hinton might be a reminder to do just this; or maybe it is saying that we slough off our sins at baptism.

(Three). If it sees a naked man it takes fright, but it will attack a clothed man. The writers draw a parallel with Adam naked in Paradise and unharmed; but outside, clothed, he becomes vulnerable. c.f. Fig.134.

The Bestiary gives us a variety of snakes some of which have been mentioned already:- Asp, Amphisbaena, the horned Cerastes, Vipers who have unnatural sexual appetites, Emorris whose poison makes us bleed to death, Dipsa which makes us die of

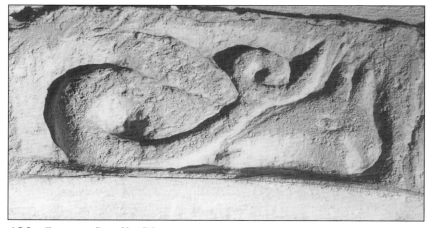

420. Lower Swell. Gloucs.
Cerastes, the horned Serpent.

thirst, Hypnale which kills by a deep sleep, Prester which induces instant putrefaction and gross swelling, Scitalis that is so brightly coloured that all top to admire it, Jaculus that throws itself from trees onto its prey, White serpents whose poison flows so fast that we are dead before we feel the bite, Seps that dissolves bones and flesh, etc. The Bestiary writer says that the horned Serpent, Cerastes; is the one in the mind of the writer of Gen 49:17. 'Dan shall be a serpent by the way an adder in the path, that biteth the horse's heels so that the rider shall fall backward.' There are many obvious possible lessons that we can learn from all these strange and frightening capabilities but it is not necessary to describe them. They are universally evil. The first three certainly appear in carvings. The others may do but it is difficult to be so certain.

The Snake as guardian spirit. The Greeks and Romans had Snake emblems as guardian spirits. Snakes and Dragons have always been the guardians of treasure. (Remember the Hobbit.) There are Snakes at the bases of columns at Bosham and on the plinths of fonts. These are guardians of the Holy Place.

Moses set up a Brazen Serpent in the wilderness on the orders of

421. Bodmin. Corn. Font.
A Peridexion Tree/Tree of Life and a mass of serpents above. Possibly the message of the plague of serpents, the brazen serpent that was raised up to heal everyone, and Christ's death on the Cross.

210

the Lord to heal people who had been bitten by the plague of fiery Serpents. Numb 21:8-9. Jesus uses the story to describe the healing, of a rather different sort, that He would bring. 'Even as Moses lifted up the serpents in the wilderness, even so must the son of Man be lifted up.' Jn 3:14. I wonder if this the thought behind the complex of coiled snakes above a Tree of Life emblem. We find examples on some Bodmin style fonts in Cornwall. (The Cross was a Tree. This Tree was the source for mankind's new life.)

BUT there is also Matt 10:16. Behold I send you forth as sheep in the midst of wolves, be ye therefore *wise* as serpents and harmless as doves.'

There are also very ancient beliefs about Serpents which include the acquisition of God like attributes and, because of their phallic shape, fertility functions. [39] There is a serpent at the base of a menhir at Carnac where it is set a foot or so in the ground. (Approx. 4000BC)

There is the Snake (or Lizard) coiled into a circle with its tail in its mouth, the Ouroboros. The spiral is in some ways similar. It is a symbol of Eternity by virtue of

422. Bosham. W.Sussex.
A Serpent guards the Holy place.

it being an endless cycle forever fading and renewing. It also expands the theme of renewal that we saw in the snake passing through a cleft in the rock.

The Serpent Nidhogg gnawed at the root of the world tree Yggdrasil in Norse mythology.

We have what amounts to a species aversion to all manner of Snake shapes. It comes as almost a relief to find that there is good in this evil form. It is wise. Under certain circumstances it can heal. It uses its power to guard the most sacred places and most valuable treasures. Nevertheless our enduring impression is of an all pervading Evil ranging over the earth but below the firmament of Heaven, as on the tympanum at Austerfield.

423. Austerfield. S.Yorks.
Satan as a Serpent ranges over the cities of the earth but below the firmament. (The thin black arc.)

[39]. Ref 53.

THE SEVEN DEADLY SINS
AND VICES GENERALLY

Pride. Wrath. Envy. Lust. Gluttony. Avarice. Sloth.

I include this short section because so many of the animals associate in some way with one or other of the Sins. Most of our Bestiary animals have a story attached to them that includes a moral to beware this or that sinful tendency. A little background information will help to set the scene.

The Seven Deadly Sins are the end product of a very long evolutionary journey. The theologies of Egypt, Babylon, and Greece plus elements from Mithraism, Gnosticism, and Zoroastrianism all have a place in this saga.[40]

424. Lincoln Cathedral.
Pride falls off his horse.

'Primitive' peoples practically everywhere believe in Demons who may be either good or evil. Human nature definitely seems to prefer tales of sin to tales of goodness and we find that the stories attached to the pictures and carvings of the Middle Ages illustrate this very well. Evil is always more dramatic and concrete in its results than good. We must propitiate the agents of Evil lest a calamity ensues. (Which of us has not 'touched wood' or 'crossed their fingers' before some risky episode.) Early Semitic peoples acknowledged the powers of seven Demons. Early Christian writers linked the Demons of antiquity with Jewish Demons. Evil Demons became the assistants of Satan. Good Demons became angels.

Christianity offered its followers a means of casting out Demons and providing protection against them.[41]

The Medieval Church found it profitable to picture Sins in cartoon form as recognisable types of men or women. Such people would be seen as inhabited by Demons. The sin, the demon and the person would thus create something more tangible and immediate than the abstract concepts that we carry today. They also believed that the Devil could actually enter into animals and change their behaviour to suit his purpose. Catholic theology had chief or Cardinal sins and Deadly or mortal sins. The Cardinal sins were the most important for one might be able to do something about them. Deadly sins lead inevitably to damnation. The first lists occur in writings from around AD 383 but were not

425. Conques. Aveyron.
Sloth, in flames, accompanied by a toad.

426. Lincoln Cathedral.
The story of Judith who tempts the enemy Holofernes then cuts off his head as he sleeps. She and her maid carry it back to the Jewish camp. The enemy panic and retreat. Virtue conquers vice.

generally adopted until the 7th or 8th Century. The Sacrament of Penance, and the needs of the confessional for an easily administered tariff, led to an early confusion of the two lists now generally known as The Seven Deadly Sins.

The Bestiaries were very popular and made it easy to find in each animal characteristics that seem appropriate to particular forms of sin. Everything in the universe had a meaning in terms of God's purpose. 'Science', which was the art of commenting on the Bible and God's creation, was an official mode for bringing His wisdom to us. The Bestiaries were the only sources for a 'Science' of

213

Natural History.

The Church disapproved of many things; gambling, playing games instead of being at study; wrestling, putting the weight and even playing the bagpipes, because it saw them as the Devil's instrument. Animals playing bagpipes are therefore indulging in a Devil inspired pursuit. All are examples of everyday activities that attracted the official Seal of Disapproval.

Pride was the most basic sin, the one from which all the others stem. Ecclesiasticus 10:13. 'For Pride is the beginning of sin and he that hath it shall pour out damnation...The Lord hath cast down the thrones of proud princes and set up the weak in their stead.' Pride heads the list; next come; Avarice / Covetousness, Luxuria (roughly the lecherous aspects of sex) (see note 9 re the tumblers at Lakenheath.) and Vanity; Anger / Despair; (The drawing of the sword indicates a desire to stab oneself and therefore despair.) Gluttony and Drunkenness; Envy; Accidie (roughly Sloth or idleness, although originally, Dryness of Spirit). Other prominent sins include Presumption, Deceit, Hypocrisy, Gossip, Gambling, and so on, all seen as offspring of the original seven. (See note 8 for an explanation of Fig.446)

I have had to make this a very brief sketch but I hope there is enough to give us an outline and a bare history of the well-known phrase. The pictures give us some idea of how the carvers interpret sins especially in relation to men and women. Each animal throughout the rest of the book also carries its own story and attribution.

[40]. See the Seven Deadly Sins. Ref 12.

[41]. Ref 13.

427. Earl Soham. Suff.
Hypocrisy prays with her eyes open.

PRIDE

428. Blythburgh. Suff.
Pride all in his fine clothes.

429. Chartres. Eure et Loir.
'Pride goes before a fall.'

430. Lincoln Cathedral.
*Alexander flies in a basket lifted by two griffins. He was so proud he
thought he could conquer and understand the mysterious heavens.*

ANGER, WRATH, DESPAIR

431. Ely Cathedral.
Domestic violence.

432. Norwich Cathedral.
Self anger or despair draws his sword to kill himself. He rides a boar.

AVARICE AND GAMBLING

433. Ely Cathedral.
Gambling.

434. Melbourne. Derbys.
Avarice, naked and still grasping his moneybag falls to his doom.

435. Wilby. Suff.
Avarice counts his money aided and abetted by a devil.

436. Lower Swell. Gloucs.
Avarice with a purse around his neck.

437. Blythburgh. Suff.
Avarice sits firmly on his money chest.

SINS OF SPEECH

438. Ludlow. Shrops.
A scold in her abominable hennin.

439. Acton. Suff.
A teller of tales.

440. Norwich Cathedral.
The Devil tempts even the King of Beasts.

441. Stratford on Avon. Warw.
'Oh, put a sock in it.'

442. Blythburgh. Suff. Poppyhead.
'Tell tale tit your tongue shall be slit.'

220

443. Cheddar. Som.
'The wicked…do whet their tongues like a sword.'
Ps.64.

444. Cheddar. Som.
The secret counsel of the wicked. Ps 64.

445. Norwich. Cathedral.
Two faced deceit.

TEMPTATION AND GLUTTONY

446. Norwich Cathedral.
A more subtle temptation; the door lies open for the devil to enter in, or for others to make easy pickings.

447. Norwich Cathedral.
The drunk glutton rides his sow.

448. Blythburgh. Suff.
The sated glutton.

449. Fairford. Gloucs.
A price to pay for overindulgence.

223

LUXURIA (Sex)

450. Wiggenhall St Germans. Norf.
'Love is blind.'

451. Barfestone, Kent.
Three attributes of lust; the Ape, the Hare and the Goat.

452. Lower Swell. Gloucs.
The 'Femme aux Serpents.' A female sinner punished through the medium of her fall.

453. Lakenheath. Suff.
Possibly a pair of homosexuals; or just acrobatic tumblers, also distracters from spiritual activity.

454. Earl Soham. Suff.
It seems the woman is always to blame.

225

SHEEP including Lamb, Wether, Ram

The Agnus Dei, the Lamb of God, is the most frequently seen image of a Sheep and I have discussed it at the beginning of this book. Sheep, Lambs and Rams, usually just a Ram's head, are fairly easy to recognise.

The Bestiary has relatively little to say about Sheep. The Lamb or the Sheep is the one amongst the faithful whose life is blameless and who obeys Mother Church. It gives us its most precious possessions, its fleece and its milk, making it a symbol of kindness and gentleness.

The Bible has very many allusions to Sheep both as a sacrificial animal and as a metaphor for the faithful. 'The Lord is my shepherd I shall not want.' Ps 23:1. 'For we like Sheep have gone astray'; from Ps 119:176. 'I am the good shepherd and know my Sheep, and am known of mine.' Jn 10:14.

Then there is the story of the original Passover. There the Israelites had to take a lamb, kill it and smear the blood on the lintel and door posts of each house. That night the Lord passes through the land to slay all the firstborn in the land of Egypt except in those houses that had the sign of the blood. These He passes over. In the same way the blood of Jesus is our passport through the otherwise inevitable destruction that follows sin.

'For even Christ our passover is sacrificed for us.' 1 Cor, 5:7. It is no coincidence that the Crucifixion happens at the time of the Feast of the Passover.

The Bible and the Bestiary both have significant stories concerning **Rams**. The Bestiary notes the head butting activities of Rams and Wethers. The writers put this down to their having worms in the head. Rams signify the Apostles or Princes of the

455. Altarnun. Corn.
A flock of Sheep. The faithful? the good? or just sheep?

Church. The Apostles have powerful foreheads with which they always overthrow whatever they strike; and they do the same with their preaching.

The main Bible story concerns the sacrifice of Isaac. This has always been seen as an allegory of the Crucifixion. God tests Abraham and asks him to offer his only son Isaac for a burnt offering. Abraham makes

Isaac carry the wood. (This is a 'Type' or Old Testament prefiguring of Christ carrying the cross.) As he is about to kill Isaac, God stays his hand. They see a Ram caught in a thicket that they use for the offering instead. (Seen as a prefiguring of Christ being sacrificed in our place for the sins of the whole world.) We quite often find an isolated Ram's head amongst the carvings inside or outside a medieval church. It is probably there to remind us of these two spiritual lessons.

There is also a Ram sign of the Zodiac...Aries; March 21st to April 19th; the first month of the year in the ancient calendar.

456. Morwenstow. Corn.
A Ram's head to remind us of Christ's sacrifice.

457. Kilpeck. H&W.
A Ram's head for a prince of the Church.

SHEILA - NA - GIG
and other sexually explicit carvings

I include these curious carvings of the female and occasionally a male, not just baring all, but doing so with relish and aggression; because they appear with animals on the outsides of churches or the holier part of the church. They occur in at least twenty-five places in the U.K. with many more in Ireland and possibly hundreds on the continent. There is not space to list all the theories about them but for a full debate see ref. 38. It must suffice to say

458. Cervatos N.Spain.
Male and female defend the east end in a fundamental way.

459. Abson. Gloucs.
A virile threat above the east window.

that they are *not* fertility goddesses left over from some Celtic or Druidic past even if some of the figures seem to be borrowed from earlier eras. Our carvers were happy to do the same with lions, peacocks and other forms giving them a totally new meaning in their new context. They are widespread from Spain to Yorkshire and Germany to Ireland, so we should not look for a very local explanation of any individual carving.

They form part of a sculptural theme in each church. Such themes spread rapidly throughout Christendom in the 1100s and 1200s. Besides females exhibiting their pudenda we find aroused or ithyphallic males in exactly similar contexts.

They and their neighbouring carvings seem to have two functions. One is a teaching or didactic programme telling us about sins against which we should be on our guard. These would include Avarice, Gluttony, Drunkenness and Luxuria or in our parlance, 'Sex.' Sex for the celibate monk meant the terrifying advances of women. It also meant homosexuality and a phallic fixation of any type whatsoever. So we find pictures of bestiality, sodomy, mutual masturbation, and sexual intercourse. They teach of matters that are too sinful to consider as befitting the spiritual life.

The other function is the 'apotropaic' one, the repelling of evil spirits and the guarding against the Evil Eye. There is a good primate zoological precedent for this in the case of the male. Some male apes will

460. Kilpeck. H&W.
A Shiela-na-gig to warn off devils.

461. Studland. Dorset.
A female defender.

sit 'on guard' with erect penises at the edge of their troop while the females and children carry on with the activities of the moment. The Greeks put up pillars known as Herms, a post with a head and erect penis, at the edge of individual plots of land. At Pompeii there are erect phalluses that have a protective rather than a 'shop sign' function.

We need not then be surprised to find many of these sexual and usually fiendish carvings on the *outside* of the church. That is the outside when it was originally built. They also appear at the entrance door or on the chancel arch, the entrance to the holiest part of God's building. They are there to warn off Devils who might be attacking the church and to terrify those who are attacking the metaphorical Church of which a humble parish church is merely the exemplar.

The most extraordinary of these sexual carvings is that of a man with his legs round his head showing not only his genitals but also an apparent vulva where his chin should

462. Bishop's Stortford. Herts.
A lady of ill repute? Or the pure person warding off sexual advances?

be. This is in a church that belonged to a nunnery. Another carving in the same church has a face half hidden by a scarf and possibly winking! We must assume the intentions of the patron were honourable

and that these are examples of vice to be avoided but I do wonder.

At Bishop's Stortford a woman with an enigmatic smile has a pair of hands making the 'fig' sign behind her head. Desmond Morris gives a list of possible present day interpretations for this sign in his book, Gestures. These vary from; 'She is an easy lay' via the idea of copulation, a general phallic gesture, a gesture of worthlessness and the apotropaic one, to a symbol of virginity. Is she a lady of easy virtue that we should avoid or is she guarding herself against the lewd advances of the opposite sex?

Sex, like any other potential vice, for example Avarice or Gluttony, becomes a real vice when indulged out of context and in undue proportion. It is also a powerful 'magic' against the unnameable forces of darkness 'out there.'

463. Swine. ER. Yorks.
Male and female pudenda in one extraordinary composition.

230

464. Beaulieu. Corrèze.
Unmonastic activity.

465. Studland. Dorset.
Intercourse as an unspiritual activity.

466. Tugford. Shrops.
A female guardian at the threshold.

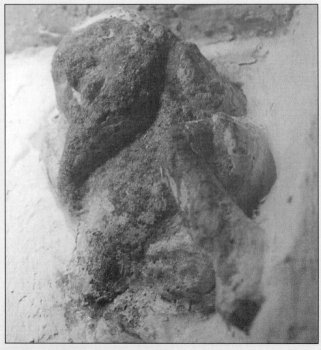

467. Tugford. Shrops.
A male guardian at the threshold. This pair are only four inches long.

SHELLS

The Scallop Shell is the attribute of St James of Compostella. It became the insignia worn by pilgrims who had undertaken the demanding journey to that far off place. Compostella in NW Spain was one of the three major pilgrimage destinations of the Middle Ages. To have travelled there was to have achieved the earthly equivalent of a major spiritual journey.

The Scallop Shell appears on tombs and effigies of local dignitaries who had presumably made the pilgrimage; or paid for someone to make it on their behalf. Wealthier people in the Middle Ages often made such payments in dedication to a saint. This was not merely a way of avoiding the difficult journey. It was more a penance for not being able to keep an earlier vow to make such a pilgrimage. It also appears in some churches like Padstow and St Mawgan-in-Pydar. These were some of the starting points for the sea journey to Spain or SW France from where most pilgrims would

468. St Mawgan in Pydar.
The scallop shell, the seamless robe and the dice the soldiers used to draw lots.

469. Norwich Cathedral.
Secure in the Faith rising to take on the Devil.

continue on foot.

There are other spiral Shells from which rise figures with a smooth or saintly look to them. It is thought that this is the newly cleansed Christian or even the Church itself, secure in the Faith and so able to take on the Devil

SIREN OR MERMAID

We should have no difficulty recognising a Mermaid but there might be more trouble with the Siren her predecessor. The Sirens are a composite of human and bird or human and fish that later evolve into our well-known Mermaid. 'Mermaids with their siren voices' are famous because they entice everyone with their songs. Mermaids have become so beautiful and so commercialised that modern society has forgotten their essentially deadly natures; for they were the medieval equivalent of a Dracula or worse.

470. Lincoln Cathedral.
The Siren as a mermaid now the nubile temptress.

471. Boston. Lincs.
Sirens lull sailors to sleep.

Ulysses had to pass the island of the Sirens and he could only do this by taking extreme precautions against temptation. He filled the sailors' ears with wax and tied himself to the mast. Had he failed the Sirens would have lulled them all to sleep then torn them limb from limb and eaten them. In Ulysses time they were Bird-Sirens. It is only later that we find an evolution into Fish-Sirens and thus our delightfully seductive Mermaids. Some even have twin tails with the possibility for a vulval orifice.

One popular perception of the time was that Mermaids were figures of prostitutes.[42]

The Mermaid of the woodcarvings usually carries a comb and a mirror in which to adjust her lovely locks: or she holds a fish in each hand. The fish is the symbol of the Christian who in this case has met his fate at the hands of the Evil One.

In three or four places we find Mermaids suckling Lions. No one so far has found the written authority for what this means. I can only suggest, but without authority, that this is an example of 'the Devil looking after his own.' (See Lam; 4:3; 'Even the sea monsters draw out the breast, they give suck to their young ones.')

[43] . Ref 34.

472. Ixworth Thorpe. Suff.
A bird Siren.

473. Stowlangtoft. Suff.
A bird - fish Siren.

234

474. Lacock Abbey. Wilts.
The true face of temptation.

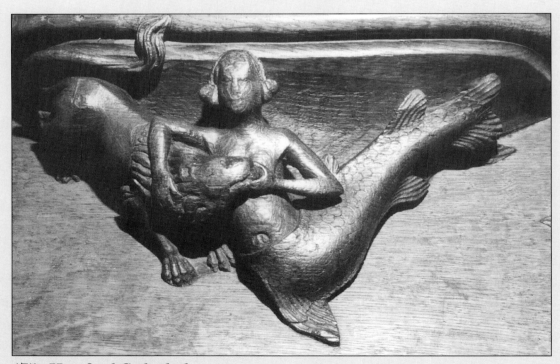

475. Hereford Cathedral.
Mermaid suckling a Lion. 'The Devil looks after his or her own.'

SLUG AND SNAIL

Snails appear in woodcarving in curious contexts. At Beverley Minster we find a man with a spear attacking one. At Bristol we have men with clubs beating a Slug.

Snails first appear in the early 1300's in the margins of illuminated manuscripts where we find them confronting an attacker. Here they seem to be involved in a parody on Cowardice, where the man has to be terribly brave to even think of attacking the Snail.[43]

Next we find the

476. Beverley Minst. ER.Yorks.
A man spears a Snail; such a worthy opponent !

477. Beverley Minst. ER.Yorks.
A man hides his head in a sack; ostrich like.

epithet 'Cowardly' attached to the Lombards of N. Italy. They had a ferocious reputation but, inexplicably, they ran away from a battle with Charlemagne in AD 772. The episode was not forgotten but became a feature of the songs of the minstrels for several hundred years.

The Lombards were the pawnbrokers and part financiers to the Medieval world. They made a good profit at this and so in both lay and clerical minds they were Usurers. A Snail, already a mental shorthand for a Coward, becomes a

236

cartoonist's way of describing the Lombards and therefore of Usurers. Usurers are guilty of Avarice probably the second most deadly of the Seven Deadly Sins. (c.f. Harpy.)

The man attacking the Snail is either someone disclosing Cowardice a derivative of the Seven Deadly Sins; or he is tackling Avarice and Usury. Interestingly the picture of the man attacking the Snail is of a misericord supporter where the other supporter shows a man burying his head in a sack. He too is afraid of something and his behaviour is also inappropriate. The centre picture on the misericord is of a man between two Dragons who have their tails wound round him. One is fierce the other is taken aback by the man who is now brave enough to put his hand in the Dragon's mouth. Is this moral fortitude in action? Has he conquered the one sin while the other still threatens?

At Villefranche-de-Rouergue, Aveyron,

478. Beverley Minst. ER.Yorks.
A man in coils of trouble; one evil is defeated, the other still threatens.

France, the anxious coward in the face in the shield has become the brave warrior with pilgrim staff, emerging from a Shell. It is a clever combination of the two concepts evoked by a Shell and the Snail.

Even the wyvern at Hereford becomes a coward in the presence of the Snail.

The Slug at Bristol may refer to the phrase a 'Sky Slug', a nickname for a slow horse in Somerset.[44] Men are beating it as they would a horse. Is this derision that they should expend so much 'valour' on such a demeaning battle?

'Four and twenty tailors went to kill a snail

The bravest man amongst them durst not touch its tail.'

The idea in this nursery rhyme seems to hark back to the associations with Cowardice that come from the Middle Ages.

I cannot find a moral meaning for the occasional Snail in carving as at Wolborough. The carver is perhaps unusually just expressing a delight in nature.

479. Wolborough. Devon.
Slug and kale. Pure natural history.

[43]. Ref 51.

[44]. Ref 55.

480. Villefranche de Rouergue. Aveyron.

The coward transformed; with his pilgrim staff and new faith, he no longer needs his pessimistic outlook.

481. Hereford Cathedral.

The Wyvern, a coward at heart, defeated by a Snail.

482. Bristol Cathedral.

A man whips a slug, (a slow horse), a pointless activity.

SPHINX

The Sphinx has a human head on a lion's body with the wings of an eagle and sometimes the hind feet of a bull. It is usually but not always female.

The Bestiary does not mention the Sphinx. Our ideas about the Sphinx seem to come from the time when Alexandria was a centre of Christian learning in the first few hundred years after the crucifixion. The Egyptian Sphinx like the Greek Sphinx guarded a secret. This was the secret for the direction of human life, and was summarised by four actions: To know, to dare, to will, to be silent. Christian teachers saw

483. Beverley Minst. ER.Yorks.
A Sphinx.

that Christ exemplified these precepts and the Sphinx became a symbol of Christ. An additional concept lay in the idea that the Sphinx, because it was a solar god, could be seen as Christ who was the light that came into the world.[45]

The four animal parts conform very closely to the four figures of the evangelists, the Tetramorph. This made another reason to give it sacred status.

Yet another sacred connection comes from the Apocryphal gospel of the acts of Andrew and Matthias. Andrew and Matthias accompany Jesus into the desert to a heathen temple which had a pair of Sphinxes at the entrance. Jesus says that these were the form of heaven; they were like the cherubim and seraphim. The Sphinxes speak to the assembled crowd pointing out how defiled they are in relation to this holy place.[46]

The Sphinx is also supposed to mean the conquest by the human spirit of animal instincts.[47]

There are a few early versions of this figure for instance at Upavon. (Fig.485 The Sphinx lies below a Pard or Mantichore.) This may relate to the series of allegories; virtues against the vices where the Sphinx is an associate of lust. The Sphinx also appears at Barfrestone below the feet of Christ. In this context it is a form of evil in subjection.

The famous riddle asks 'What goes on four feet, on two feet and on three?' The answer is 'Man' who crawls as a child, walks upright as an adult and uses a stick in old age. Oedipus had to answer this riddle before passing on to marry the queen. She was his mother though neither of them knew it. He had unknowingly already killed his father.

The Sphinx may represent wisdom as exemplified in Christ and all that He taught. She may represent evil and especially a fear of the unknown because she is still inscrutable and an enigma. I find her meaning the most difficult to define of all 'God's Beasts.'

484. Beverley Minst. ER.Yorks.
A Sphinx.

485. Upavon. Wilts.
A Sphinx joins a Mantichore or possibly a Pard

Other beasts that we may confuse with the Sphinx include Harpies and Lamia.

[45]. Ref 16.

[46]. Ref 37.

[47]. Ref 20.

SQUIRREL

Squirrels are such common animals that I think we might excuse ourselves if we just accept carvings of them at face value as pleasant examples of local craftsmanship. They are easy to recognise. However even Squirrels had a moral meaning according to the later Bestiaries. They say that when it wishes to cross a stream it jumps on a piece of wood and crosses the water using its tail as a sail. (Possibly the origin for the Squirrel Nutkin story?). They draw an analogy with the Christian who needs to hold on to the Cross while traversing the troubled seas of Life. They also say that when hunted it rushes for the tree tops. This should be the pattern for a Christian who has little security in things of the earth but much safety in the loftier places of heavenly meditation.

At Bakewell there is a Squirrel at the upper end of the upright of a Cross, while beneath a man aims an arrow upwards. This is a very early carving and may relate to a Norse legend. In this the Squirrel tries to annoy the Gods so that they would engage in

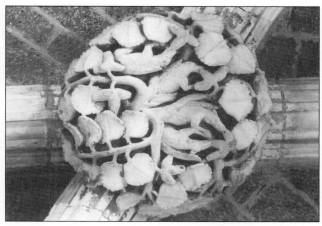

486. Exeter Cathedral. Ambulatory.
Squirrels feed on God given food.

warfare and bring on Rangnarok, the end of the world. So this may be an evil Squirrel being shot by the Good Christian or by Christ

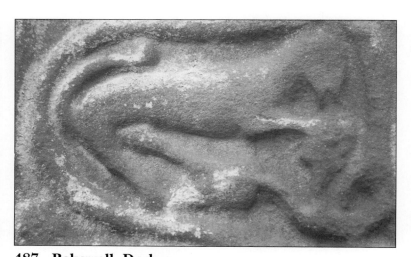

487. Bakewell. Derbys.
The top of the shaft for a cross. A Squirrel despoils the food; below a man aims an arrow upwards. (out of picture)

488. Salle. Norf.
A Squirrel enjoys the good things of the spiritual life.

STORK and see Heron and Crane

Storks are virtually indistinguishable from cranes and carry a broadly positive symbolism very similar to that of the crane and heron. The Bestiary says that the parents take extremely good care of their young. The young reciprocate this care in their turn. They signify prudent men, the careful servants of God. The Stork pursues snakes to draw off poison and good men pursue evil spirits to reduce their evil ideas to nothing.

489. N. Cadbury. Som.
A Stork or a Heron.

SWAN

Most Swans in carvings are very obvious because of their long necks. However there are some birds with short necks that are certainly Swans. There are others that probably represent Swans because the geese or ducks that they vaguely resemble carry no spiritual message.

Swans, the Bestiaries say, sing most beautifully; the curve of the neck in particular gives great variety and beauty of tone to their utterances. (Strange, when we call them mute swans.) A Swan, when it dies, sings

490. Exeter Cathedral.
Tomb of Hugh Courtenay and his wife, a De Bohun. A Heraldic but also dying pair of Swans, with echoes of the good Christian life

its sweetest song. This is the origin of our phrase, 'a Swan Song', and understandably a Swan can appear as an attribute of any Christian martyr.

The Bestiary also points out that Swans have white feathers but black flesh. In this instance it is an example of a hypocrite. (Fig.492). It adds that, as the Swan when stripped of its feathers, is roasted; so too the proud will be stripped of their pomp and roasted in hell.

We often find heraldic Swans in church carvings. They are likely to be either the device of the De Bohun family, one of the original great families that came over with the Conqueror; or a badge for Bishop Hugh of Lincoln who had a pet Swan that accompanied him during his life.

All three elements The Dying Swan, a

Christian Martyr, the De Bohun heraldic emblem combine most beautifully on the tomb of Hugh Courtenay and his wife, a De Bohun, in Exeter Cathedral.

A Swan features in the Lohengrin saga, which appears in some Church carvings. For the story of the Lohengrin Swan see under Fables.

243

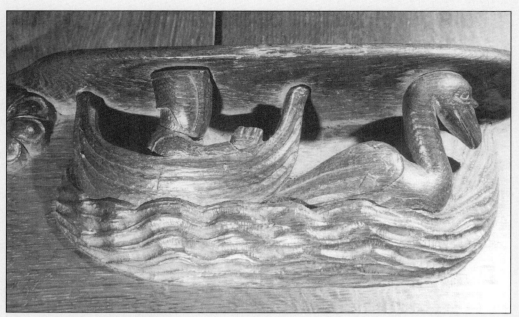

491. Exeter Cathedral.
The Lohengrin Swan; (see fables).

492. Rodez. Aveyron.
The Swan as hypocrite; white feathers but black skin.

TERREBOLEM OR FIRE STONES

Terrebolem or Terrobuli are some of the most extraordinary of the items that we find in the Bestiaries. They were stones that were either male or female and that exist on an oriental mountain. So long as they are far apart all is well. However when the female approaches the male, flames burst out and the mountain catches fire. So, the Bestiary says, O Men of God, keep well away from women; lest the flame break out in you and burn up the good things which Christ has conferred upon you.

493. Alne. N.Yorks.
A Pair of Terrebolem surrounded by flames.

They are difficult to recognise. They are surprisingly rare in sculpture considering the dangers they thought sexual attraction posed to progress in the spiritual life.

The curious paired figures at Witherfield are Terrebolem according to my reading. It is difficult to see what else they could be, but they are certainly not as clear a portrayal of male and female stones as the pictures in the Bestiary. (Note 10.)

494. Withersfield. Essex.
A pair of Terrebolem in coils of trouble.

TETRAMORPH

The Tetramorph or four shapes or forms refers to the four animal symbols of the Evangelists. The early Fathers arrived at a consensus about AD 400 as to which animal represented which Evangelist. The Bible references are Ezek 1: 5-11 and Rev 4: 6-7. The latter says '...round about the throne were four beasts full of eyes before and behind. And the first beast was like a lion, and the second beast was like a calf, and the third beast had the face of a man, and the fourth beast was like a flying eagle...'

495. Chartres. Eure et Loir.
Christ surrounded by the four symbols of the evangelists.

If we now consider the first chapter of each gospel we find how the early Fathers made the allocation. *St Matthew's Gospel* begins with that long genealogy of Christ so his symbol became that of a Man. We find this usually shown as a Man with wings that we tend to interpret as an angel though strictly speaking this is incorrect. *St Mark's* Gospel begins with story of John the Baptist, one crying in the wilderness. Lions come from the wilderness so it was appropriate for the Lion to belong to St Mark.

St Luke's Gospel starts with the story of Zacharias, a priest, offering incense at the time Gabriel tells him that his wife will conceive. His duties would have included arranging sacrifices in the temple. A Calf or a Bull is a sacrificial animal, which thus became St. Luke's emblem. *St John's* Gospel begins 'in the beginning was the Word, and the Word was with God and the Word was God.' We move straight into the presence of the Almighty. Only Eagles can fly very high and look undazzled on the sun, here used as a metaphor for God. Hence the Eagle becomes the emblem of St John. For similar reasons we have Eagle lecterns. The lectern carries the Bible the Word of God. It is into God's presence that the Eagle takes us with his precious load.

496. Elkstone. Gloucs.
Christ plus the four symbols of the evangelists with an Agnus Dei and the hand of the Father reaching down from above.

TIGER

As with crosswords where it is sometimes possible to find an answer and then work out why it should fit the clue, so some very curious carvings turn out to be of a Tiger, for which the clue is the following story from the Bestiary.

A hunter sets out to capture some Tiger cubs. He knows that in the normal course of events he will never escape from such an

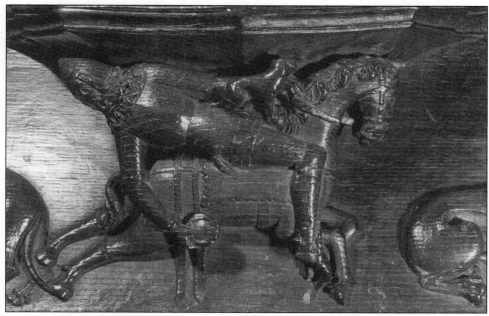

497. Chester Cathedral.
The capture of the Tiger cub. Our soul is carried off by Satan.

498. Wendens Ambo. Essex.
The Tigress delayed by the glittering shams of the world, as in this mirror.

undertaking, so he takes a mirror or crystal ball with him with which he hopes to divert the Tigress. He finds and seizes a cub and when chased by the Tigress, throws down the mirror. Her reflection fools the Tigress into thinking that she has her cub safely returned to her and so she stops the chase. Meanwhile the hunter makes his escape.

The moral of the story is that we Christians are the

Tigress; the cubs are our souls. The hunter is the Devil who will carry our souls off to Hell if we allow the vain pomp and glittering shams of this world to distract us.

Some of the examples are most unlike a Tiger, for instance the carving at Wendens Ambo. Bear in mind that it is the story that matters not zoological accuracy of representation.

499. Lakenheath. Suff.
A Tigress distracted by seeing her face in a mirror.

500. Badingham. Suff. On the roof.
A Tiger delays just too long.

Illust. 12.
The Tiger story in the Bestiary.

248

TREE OF LIFE
TREE OF KNOWLEDGE OF GOOD & EVIL
TREE OF THE CROSS
PERIDEXION TREE

I include a short section on The Tree because so very many of the animals are entwined in foliage or eating it, or sometimes extruding it. It is important to consider the subject if only to help with the context of such carvings; and The Peridexion Tree always has an evil Dragon beneath it.

501. Kilpeck H&W. Tympanum.
The Tree of Life. 'I am the true vine.' Christ is the door to the spiritual life. c.f. Fig.201.

The phrase 'Tree of Life' is so common, if not quite in everyday speech certainly in church leaflets that one tends to accept it without exploring the ideas it is trying to convey. It would be impossible in even a large book to outline all the strands of the Tree of Life story. Some concepts are vital and this is a rapid run through of some of the most important.

The Tree at the centre of the world is an idea almost as old as civilisation itself; certainly from several thousand years BC. The Tree has roots that go down to the underworld, a trunk and lower branches in this world, and leaves in the upper heavenly worlds. The Scandinavian Yggdrasil or World Tree is close to this concept. The Tree as an axis for the world and as a centre for an ascent to heaven is a concept given physical form in the Buddhist stupa. A pole rises through seven layers representing the seven heavens.

Some animals have foliage coming from their mouths. It is helpful to see this as Life, the new spiritual Life.

Some animals eat the foliage; they seek for healing from a special herb, Dittany. The Tree of Life also provides healing in the broadest sense and is fodder for goats in many early medieval sculptures. In that sense it is an equivalent for Dittany. The

Foliage, besides healing people was seen as the food for Our Lord and this foliage is the faithful congregation of all Christian people. (See p.97) The foliage of the Tree both Heals and Sustains.

There is apparent death followed by renewal and rebirth in deciduous trees; a cycle recalled in the Green Man stories.

In the Bible there are two trees in Genesis. There is *The Tree of Knowledge of Good and Evil*, the fruit of which Adam and Eve partook with such disastrous

502. Dinton. Bucks.
To him that overcometh will I give to eat of the Tree of Life.' Rev.2;7.

consequences. The story appears in Gen. Ch. 2&3. Then there is the *Tree of Life*, Gen 3:22. 'The Lord God said "Behold the man has become like one of us, knowing good and evil: and now, lest he put forth his hand and take also of the Tree of Life, and eat, and live forever." Therefore the Lord God sent him forth from the Garden of Eden, to till the ground from which he was taken.'

Legend has it that a seed saved from the Tree was planted in the mouth of Adam when he died and from this sprang the Tree from which they made the Cross. We sometimes find The Cross pictured as a Tree with stubby branches and incipient foliage. Christ died on the Tree in order to give us New Life. The foliage that spews from the mouths of what look to us like fearsome heads on Norman archways, is the foliage of New Life or Heavenly Life. It will later join with and evolve into the foliage of the Green Man; another metaphor for the source of New Life. (Fig.201 Kilpeck. This is the same foliage as in Kilpeck's Tree of Life. Fig.501)

At the end of Time and at the end of the Bible the *Tree of Life* appears again. 'This tree bare twelve manner of fruits and the leaves were for the healing of the nations.' Rev 22:2. It stood in 'a pure river of the water of life, clear as crystal, proceeding out of the throne of God.' (Fig.502)

503. Bishops Lydeard. Som.
The Green Man and The Tree.

This is Paradise achieved at last. The Tympanum at Dinton describes the route to it so well. Two animals eat of the fruit of the Tree of Life. Below it says 'If any despair of obtaining reward for his desserts let him attend to the doctrines here preached and take care to keep them in mind.'

The Bestiary talks of a *Peridexion or Perindens Tree*. This tree grows in 'India', that mysterious land of the East. It has very sweet fruit and doves delight to feed and rest in it. The Dragon who is the enemy of the doves, cannot approach the Tree or its shadow and he must prowl around below. The Tree is God the Father. The fruit is Christ. The shadow is the Holy Spirit. The Doves are ourselves. The moral being that if you have the Holy Spirit the Devil cannot come near you. However the Devil will surely devour you if you venture outside the shadow and therefore outside Holy Church. The Bestiary illustration is of a Tree with fierce Dragons at the foot looking expectantly into the branches. The font at Bodmin shows this very well. East Meon has a more stylised version while the misericord at Ripon loses the Tree altogether. They all tell the same story; if you are baptised and follow the commandments of God, you will be assured of a place in Paradise.

504. Bishops Lydeard. Som.
The Pelican, a picture of our salvation, nests in the Tree.

The Pelican is in a Tree at Bishops Lydeard where also the Green Man and the Tree join in a common symbolism. Fig.503.

505. East Meon. Hants. Font.
Dragons cannot reach birds in the Peridexion Tree or its shadow.

251

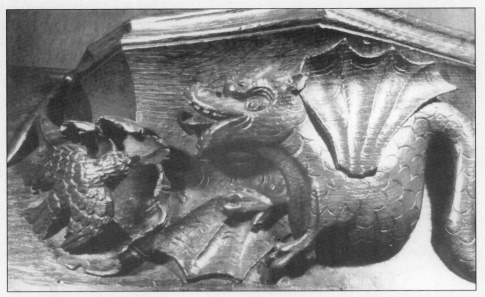

506. Ripon. N.Yorks.

Christian souls (birds) safe from Satan (Wyvern) while they remain in the foliage.

507. Bodmin. Corn.

Two dragons patrol around the base of a Peridexion tree.

Illust. 13.

The Peridexion Tree

TUTIVILLUS

He has a curious awkward name that one might know better as Shakespeare's 'Titivally'. He is one of the few named minions of the Devil with his own very specific job description. His task was to listen for idle chatter, gossip, and slander in church, as well as taking note of mumbled prayers or mistakes in the liturgy made by the Parson. He notes down all these misdemeanours on a long screed that he saves in a sack until the dreadful Day of Judgement. He or his acolytes carry the sack and quill pen.

We often find him peering over the heads of women where he acts as a spy for the Devil. He features with Bell, Book and Candle, the means for his excommunication, on a bench end at Charlton Mackrell, except that here the carver has mistakenly given him a flower instead of a candle. He is always repulsive and rather frightening.

508. Charlton Mackrell. Som.
Tutivillus with his pen, scroll and sack stubs his toe on bell, book and candle. (candle misdrawn as a flower.) the instruments of his demise.

509. Minster in Thanet. Kent.
Tutivillus hides in the ladies head-dress.

510. Enville. staffs.
Tutivillus listens for idle chatter and mumbled prayers.

UNICORN

We would all agree that the Unicorn is a mythical animal yet advertisers and others still use it to evoke thoughts of strength, freedom, purity and other associated ideas. Such modern notions leave us with a very poor image of what the Unicorn meant to medieval churchgoers.

The Bestiary writers knew of two animals with a single horn. One is the Unicorn the other a Monoceros. The Monoceros is an animal like a rhino for it had elephant's feet. The Unicorn is more like a goat but they say it is called rhinoceros. They certainly had a fairly clear mental image of two different animals. Inevitably the characteristics and meaning of each became blurred and merged into each other. The

511. Greystoke. Cumb.
The capture of the Unicorn. Christ, born of the flesh and the Spirit; dies in the flesh, to rise in the Spirit.

point about the Unicorn was that it was so fierce that no one could take it alive except in one circumstance.

The story that became attached to the Unicorn in the Middle Ages concerns this capture. There were two methods. The most popular lay in the fact that the Unicorn would lay its head in the lap of a virgin and only a virgin. So they place a virgin in the forest. The Unicorn duly places his noble head on her lap, when the hunter may easily kill it. In the alternative method the hunter tempts the Unicorn to charge then jumps behind a tree at the last moment. The Unicorn plunges its horn into the tree trunk and is then easily caught. (Fig.512) The tree is in water giving a double symbolism of spiritual death followed by rebirth through baptism.

The usual interpretation of these stories is that the Unicorn is Christ, the Virgin is the Virgin Mary and the Hunter is God the

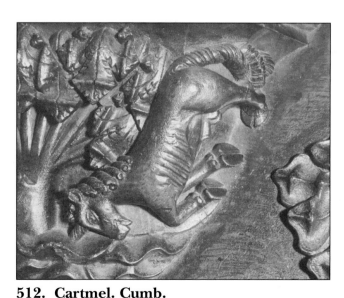

512. Cartmel. Cumb.
A Unicorn captured when it plunges its horn into a tree.

Father. Christ becomes flesh through the offices of the Virgin but is condemned to a physical death. Alternatively the emphasis is put on the fact that Christ the Unicorn is Incarnate by the Virgin Mary yet willingly surrenders to the Jews who sought Him. If we hold to these two concepts we shall gain most of the spiritual message that all the Unicorn carvings are trying to tell us.

One Bestiary in Padua gives a totally different meaning. The Unicorn is a symbol of violent and cruel people, who only the Grace of God can subdue.[48] This is an unlikely interpretation for most carvings that we shall meet with in our churches.

The word Unicorn occurs in the Bible in Num 23:22 and Deut 33:17 where it is used as an allegory for God's great strength. In the later Middle Ages and Renaissance the Unicorn became part of the symbolism of perfect love and of chastity. These are ideas that we associate with the romance of chivalry. The very beautiful Unicorn tapestries from this later period are full of

513. Barwick. Som. *The Unicorn as Christ from whom grows a Tree of Life with pomegranate for fruit. The seeds are (i) the faithful held together in the body of the Church and (ii) one of the joys of heaven being a fruit promised to the Children of Israel when they would reach the promised land.*

the most delightful and complex symbols. We should not however take all those symbols to heart when looking at medieval carvings in churches, for their associations and meanings are secular in origin not theological

The horn also acquired great therapeutic powers. It could detect poison, or so they thought, and the very wealthy used it for this very purpose. The horn (pieces of Narwhal horn) was literally worth more than its weight in gold.

514. Stowlangtoft. Suff.
A Unicorn ready unto death ?

[48]. Ref 53.

VULTURE

The Bestiaries illustrate Vultures in pairs with necks or bodies crossed so it is reasonably safe to assume that these are Vultures at Carlisle. Likewise the birds attacking an animal body at Whalley bear a strong resemblance to the Vultures in M.S.Bodley 764.[49]

Vultures were famed for being able to conceive without carnal knowledge of the other sex. They were therefore an example to doubters of Mary's virginity, that indeed such things were possible; and that 'the Lord who is our flesh will affirm the truth.'

515. Carlisle. Cumb.
A broken pair of Vultures. They reproduce without carnal knowledge. An example from nature to doubters of Mary's virginity.

The writers acknowledge that they had keen eyesight and an uncanny knack of knowing where and when a bloody battle would take place but they drew no lessons from this for us.[50]

[49]. Ref 8.

[50]. A boss Exeter; E.end, S.aisle, has a bird attacking a pig's stomach like the birds do at Whalley. The pig is a shorthand for Jew. The bird could well be a Vulture; here Mary feeding on her Jewish ancestry. Alternatively it may be a bird of prey, giving the composition an anti-Jewish slant like the birds that mob owls.

516. Whalley. Lancs.
Two Vultures feed on a dead lamb.

WHALE

The only Biblical Whale is the one that swallowed Jonah. There are other large fish of various descriptions but unless the picture shows one actually swallowing Jonah, we should not call it a Whale. The Bestiary barely mentions the Whale and makes no moral point about the animal's great size.

There are several important points in the Jonah story. Jesus uses the legend about Jonah's adventure inside the Whale to foretell His own descent into the heart of the earth. Matt 12:40. 'For as Jonas was three days and three nights in the

517. Ripon. N.Yorks.
Jonah cast overboard.

Whale's belly, so shall the son of Man be three days and nights in the heart of the earth.' The Jonah and the Whale story affirm for us that Christ's death and Resurrection were more than mere incidents in history. They were pre-ordained. This is one of the stories that the medieval theologian uses as confirmation that the Old Testament truly has many lessons that we can only understand when we have a knowledge of the New.

The other fish that cause confusion with the Whale are the Aspidochelone, the Dolphin, the Serra and Leviathan.

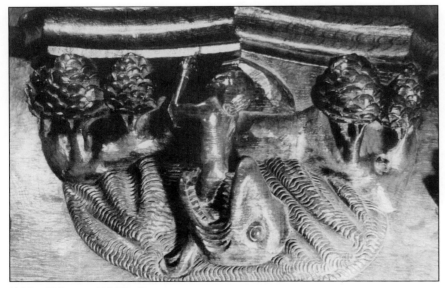

518. Ripon. N.Yorks.
Jonah delivered up by the Whale.

THE WILD MAN OR WOODWOSE

The name Wild Man describes two rather different beings. One is a naked man struggling to acquire a Lion's skin. The other is a large strong man dressed in fur who holds a mighty club. There are essentially two distinct stories about these people and they are very different from one another.

Firstly the spiritual story. There were Wild hairy men living in 'India'; that is to the Medieval mind far away in a mysterious east.

519. Hereford Cathedral.
The Wild Man seeks the Lion's skin.

These hairy men were perpetually at war with a tribe called the Sagittarii. The Wild Man had to move around naked and was therefore at a disadvantage in this fight until he had slain a Lion and could wear the skin. One of the Sagittarii represents Man's body. The Wild Man represents his soul. They war with each other until the soul gains enough strength from the Lion's skin to slay the body, and with it, the power of the vain delights of this world.[51] Gaining the Lion's skin is equivalent in modern parlance to being 'saved' and also bears comparison to Paul's admonition to put on the whole armour of God. Eph. 6:11 and Rom.13:12. We should remind ourselves of this story whenever we see a naked man, or one man versus a Lion, or a man with Lion's skin and a club, looking rather pleased with himself.

The second collection of stories all hark back to a 'Wild Man of the Woods' concept.

This was someone who was brutish with a great strength that came from the lapse of all the usual controls. He was unpredictable, uncultured, unintelligible, strong and lustful. His great strength can be used to guard the house and protect the family escutcheon. They draw or carve him with a mighty club and dressed as he would have been for a Medieval play. He protects the doorways of Town Halls as well as churches. He proudly carries his masters Coat of Arms. There are many examples especially in E. Anglia, but it is difficult to give him a moral or spiritual significance in these contexts. Maybe he is God's bouncer protecting the holy and special places in this world.[52]

[51]. Ref 3. p182.

[52]. Ref 11.

258

520. Beverley St Mary. ER.Yorks.
The Wild Man triumphant.

521. Norton. Suff. Font.
The Wild Man guards the font and bears the family shield.

259

WOLF

A Wolf bites his paw unless it is the Wolf that guards St Edmund's head. If there are other Wolves I have yet to recognise them. It was very cunning in hunting, always coming upwind, and should it snap a twig it would bite the offending foot as punishment. It is this image that the carvers use to indicate that we are looking at a Wolf.

All the negative images that we associate with the Wolf are but a fraction of those that would have been current to the minds of medieval men and women. We talk of a Wolf in sheep's clothing and know the sexual hopes of the man making a Wolf whistle. For people for whom the Wolf was

522. Faversham. Kent.
A Wolf licks a careless paw.

an everyday intruder and destroyer of their carefully conserved flocks, the rapacious nature of Wolves needed little explanation.

The Bible reminds us 'to beware of false prophets which come to you in sheep's clothing but inwardly they are ravening Wolves.' Matt 7:15. The behaviour of some in Holy Orders was clearly unacceptable and people undoubtedly saw them as just such Wolves. They join the aristocracy in the Reynard stories. Tax collectors, bailiffs, and those of similar money collecting and property despoiling professions carry the same tag.

We have lost the use of 'Wolf' for Prostitute but it

523. Les Andelys. Eure.
A Wolf punishes the noisy leg.

was a current epithet from Roman to Elizabethan times. The Bestiary uses this image saying that whores are called She Wolves because they destroy the wealth of their lovers. Like the hyena it was supposed not to be able to bend the neck back.

There were other little faults. If a wolf saw a man before the man saw him, the man would lose his voice and the Wolf need have no more fear of him. Its eyes shone in the darkness; and in just such a way may the Devil blind foolish men.

The Danes slew St Edmund and there is one good Wolf who guards the head until it can be given

524. Iffley. Oxon.
A Wolf punishes an erring member.

Christian burial. This is a common image in East Anglia where St. Edmund was very much the local hero.

There are only a few Wolf carvings so I have included one from France that shows that he bites a paw. It also demonstrates the curious Bestiary convention that animals were three toed, even though they must have known that in real life they had proper claws.

525. Hadleigh. Suff.
A Wolf takes charge of St Edmund's head.

WYVERN

Wyverns are two legged dragons and very popular with our carvers. Dragons have four legs and maybe are that much more difficult to carve. Certainly symbolically there is nothing to choose between them and all that they say about Dragons can apply here. They are totally evil, fierce, rapacious, and deadly and give a wonderful idea of the fate awaiting the wrongdoer.

526. Dunblane. Stirling.
A fierce Wyvern.

527. Stowlangtoft. Suff.
A very handsome Wyvern spotted with sin.

528. Ripon. N.Yorks.
A Wyvern frustrated because the sheep are safe in the shade of the Peridexion Tree.

YALE OR EALE

The Bestiary says that the Yale is as big as a horse with boar like jaws and the tail of an elephant. It had rather special horns that it could swivel backwards or forwards at will. In a fight it keeps one horn pointed back to act as a spare should the first be broken. It has no moral significance and so is rare in carvings. It does feature in heraldry notably in the arms of Lady Margaret Beaufort, mother of King Henry VII. We can see it on the entrance gate of Christ's College, Cambridge. It appears in the roof of nearby Burwell and on a shield at N. Cadbury, where its significance is heraldic.

529. N. Cadbury. Som.
The Yale.

NOTES

1. This story was obviously part of general folklore in Shakespeare's time for he refers to it on two occasions. Katherine, in The Taming of the Shrew,(II.1.32.) says that she will have to lead Apes in Hell all because the man she loves prefers Bianca; that is, Katherine will end up an Old Maid.
Beatrice, in Much Ado,(II.1.40) tells Leonato her uncle what he can do with his suggestions for suitors. 'therefore I will take sixpence in earnest of the bear'ard and lead Apes into hell.'

2. Daniel with Bel and the Dragon.
On Daniel's right the lion turns away as if no longer posing a threat. Daniel's left hand is definitely in the Lion or Dragon's mouth on the tympanum at Down St. Mary. There are other, later pictures that use the same action with probably the same intent. See under Snail in this book. They illustrate in a general way the principle of victory over the evil power. There is a Bible illustration that uses the same idea. Is.11:8. 'The sucking child shall play on the hole of the Asp and the weaned child shall put his hand in the Cockatrice's den.' It is part of Isaiah's prophecy of Victory following Christ's arrival. The message is the same whether we read the animal as Lion or as Dragon; the power of the animal has been tamed.

3. At Dinton the picture is usually stated to be St Michael on the right attacking the fiery Dragon on the left. Fiery dragons should have multiple fiery 'tongues'. In this carving St Michael is using the pointed foot of the cross in his right hand to kill the serpent at his feet. This is the way in which, in every other carving of the same subject, he disposes of the Dragon. The Dragon on the left has a large smooth 'tongue'. I think that these two pictures are in parallel and telling the same story. The Dragon on the left is a crocodile swallowing a large smooth Hydrus that we have seen represents Christ destroying Satan in Hell. On the right we have St Michael conquering the Serpent that tells the same story and reinforces the totality of the conquest of Evil. St Michael is present with Christ in Hell when he binds Satan for a thousand years; in the story of the Harrowing of Hell.

4. On many arches of Norman churches there are curious and often monstrous heads apparently swallowing all sorts of lesser or more normal beings. If we look carefully not all of them are swallowing these people; some are *disgorging* them. This is not an idea with which we have grown up but it does fit the story on the arch very well. It is about the end of time when the dead are delivered up for Judgement and everlasting bliss. Some of the heads on Norman arches and sometimes the corbels that have heads or torsos apparently within their jaws may be such beasts. Others are definitely Satanic swallowing sinners of one sort or another. The heads that appear to swallow whole pillars are also possibly better viewed as god like beings extruding the foundations of the Church.[53]

5. The Picardy Bestiary says that the Lioness brings forth a piece of flesh resembling a Lion through her mouth. The Father Lion brings it to life on the third day by breathing on it.[54] This description is such an exact match for the figure on the font at Melbury Bubb that I feel the carver must have known of it.

6. At Fritwell, Oxon.; there are two Leonine animals separated by what looks like a candle. Green foliage comes from their mouths. The animal on the right has

Lion markings so the one on the left should be a Panther whose bright colouring has long since worn away. Neither are eating of the Tree of Life, they are, if anything producing it. Compare Milborne Port and Eversdon, Yorks.

7. In A Midsummer Night's Dream, Act III Titania falls in love with Bottom when he is dressed in an Ass's head. I wonder if the crowd at The Globe would have appreciated the possible rather lewd inference in this curious fixation of the Fairy Queen's?

8. The carving of a castle with a door ajar as at Norwich cathedral has been a puzzle but I believe there is a clue to an explanation in a picture in Speculum Humanae Salvationis. In Ch. XIII, Christ is shown being tempted by Satan in the wilderness. In one part of this picture Christ is on the upper ramparts of a building, (the pinnacle of the temple) admonishing the

530. Fritwell. Oxon.

A Lion (Rt) and maybe Panther (Lt) beside a Light of the world (?)

tempter. There is a door ajar in the lower wall. The open door of the castle, that has distinct similarities with this picture, is a Temptation to the opportunist thief or usurper to enter and take possession. Exactly the same carving occurs at Montreal. Yonne. France.

9. The carving of two tumblers intertwined where unfortunately more than half the carving has been cut away, has possible homoerotic connotations. There is definitely a 'kiss my arse' appearance to the remaining head and buttocks. Both tumblers and homosexuals would have attracted the displeasure of the Church and this could depict either. I know of no other carvings of similar tumblers in this country. There are some of rather similar homosexual acts, though not in this country.

10. The Withersfield figures (Fig.494) have possible antecedents in a Bestiary in Westminster Abbey Library. MS 22, f.54.[55].

11. There are places in France where one can see the same idea. At Neuilly en Donjon, (Loire), a tympanum shows the Epiphany.

531. Montreal. Yonne.

An open door to the fortress; an invitation to the devil to enter. (compare Norwich Fig.446)

Angels sound trumpets and the wise men present themselves to the infant Jesus. Beneath their feet lie two beasts one a big cat with large spots on his feet, the other a cloven footed animal with tiny horns. I believe that these are the Leopard and the Kid. They too have small wings which has led some people to say that they are two of the beasts that represent the evangelists, the lion and the ox. Or, alternatively that they are non-specific beasts representing sin. The animal with little horns looks very like a kid and no lion has claws like this one. It makes much more sense to see it as an illustration of Isaiah 11:6. Other symbols of the age of Innocence occur possibly at Kilpeck where a hare and hound look out expectantly from the east end of the church. Analogous symbols appear on misericords such as at Rodez (Fig.403) where a cat and a dog share the same basket and at Bakewell, (Fig.374) These are three hundred years later. The idea is the same but it is expressed

532. Neuilly en Donjon. Allier.
The Epiphany. The three kings greet Mary and the infant Jesus. The angels announce this great moment. The Leopard lies down with the Kid. (Is.11.)

in a more down to earth fashion. None except Rodez, so far as I can discover, have been recognised and described with this meaning. (Figs.532, 533, 534.)

[53]. Ref R.W. of 62 Personal comm.

[54]. Ref 52. p343.

[55]. Ref 34.

533. Neuilly en Donjon. Allier.
The Kid.

534. Neuilly en Donjon. Allier.
The Leopard.

267

SHORT CUTS

This is neither foolproof nor comprehensive. The crucial detail will introduce us to the significant aspect of the picture. From there we may recognise a similarity and with luck proceed to the correct answer.

Animal biting foot
is likely to be a   Wolf

Bird biting foot
is likely to be a   Peacock

Animal with a large tongue
is likely to refer to   Hydrus

Animal with round smooth
object in mouth,   Crocodile &
or facing a round object   Hydrus

Animal with a head in its mouth
may be a   Hyena

Animal with a head coming
out of its mouth,
may be a Personification of the Deep Sea
where this head is more out than in.

'Dragon' with forked tail
is likely to be a   Salamander

'Dragon' with knotted tail
is likely to be a   Salamander

Cock with serpent tail
is likely to be a   Basilisk

Dog like animal
attending to private parts
 is likely to be a   Beaver

'Hound' with a round dish
is likely to be a   Tiger

Animal with a prominent spine
is likely to be a   Hyena

'Lion' with a cone of breath
is likely to be a   Panther

'Lion' with a large
protruding tongue, full face
is likely to be a   Pard

'Lion' with a human face
is likely to be a   Mantichore

Winged fish
is likely to be a   Serra

Fish swallowing another fish
is likely to be an   Aspidochelone

A head at both ends
is likely to be an   Amphisbaena

Triple face
see under   Harpy

CONCEPTS

This includes a miscellany of the symbols, and ideas behind the symbols, that we deal with in this book. There are so many ways of viewing even one symbol that I do not attempt to make a comprehensive list. Rather it is a quick guide to some of the ideas to which the carvings refer.

Avarice.
Harpy. Ape as doctor. Bel and Dragon. Three in one face.

Baptism.
Eagle. Hydrus. Elephant. Salamander. Serpent. Boar and Hunter. Partridge. Mole.

Better followers of the Christian life.
Beaver. Lizard. Hart or Deer. Heron. Hoopoe. Salamander.

Chastity.
Beaver. Elephant. Unicorn.

Christ.
Hydrus. Goat. Lion. Panther. Pelican. Phoenix. Green Man. Lamb. Stag or Hart. Cancer/Crab. Unicorn.

Christ opening Gates of Hell.
Samson and Lion. David and Lion. Crocodile and Hydrus. David and Goliath. Jonah and Whale. Centaur v Leviathan / Dragon. Sagittarius. Daniel in the Lion's den. Moses leading children of Israel out of Egypt.

Christian Unity.
Bat.

Deceit.
Amphisbaena. Crocodile. Ape.
Envy.
Dog with a bone.

Eucharist.
Pelican. Birds in the vine. Doves and Chalice. Birds and corn.

Faithfulness.
Dog.

Gentiles
Raven.

Gluttony and Drink.
Antelope. Bear. Boar. Pig.

Guardians.
Griffins. Lions.Serpents.

Heresy.
Cat.

Homosexual.
Partridge.

Humility
Camel

Hypocrisy.
Crocodile. Swan.

Jews.
Pigs. Owls. Harpies. Hyena.

Liberality.
Cock and Hen.

'Life'
Foliage coming from the mouth of heads, faces, animal faces especially lions, and foliage embracing subjects in a benevolent way. Jn. 10:10 'I am come that they may have Life.'

Lust.
Ape. Basilisk. Bear. Boar. Camel. Centaur. Goat. Hare.

Madness as part of Wrath.
Swine.

Parthenogenesis. That is asexual reproduction.
Hence the **Incarnation.**
Hare. Vulture.

Penance and Confession.
Raven.

Prostitute.
Basilisk. Ape. Wolf. Siren/Mermaid.

Resurrection.
Phoenix. Peacock. A sea animal giving up the dead.

Salvation.
Dolphin. Elephant. Pelican. Woodwose. Goat feeding on Dittany. Hares. Rabbits. Foxes.

Satan.
Asp. Basilisk. Aspidochelone. Boar. Cat. Crocodile. Frog. Hedgehog. Hyena. Lizard. Mantichore. Lion. Pard. Leopard. Crossbills. Parrots. Partridge. Fox. Wolf. Salamander. Scorpion. Serpent. Dragon. Wyvern.

Shame.
Peacock.

Sinners.
Raven. Pig.

Timid Christian.
Ibis.

Vigilance.
Cock. Amphisbaena. Crane.

Virgin Mary.
Elephant. Hare. The Virgin in the Unicorn story. Vulture.

Wise Men.
Ibex

CONCLUSION

This book is only a beginning. There are still many carvings we do not understand. We are now in a better position to 'weigh possible alternatives' before letting ourselves 'be led into heavenly hierarchies' which was the original purpose of the carvings. Our faith may have difficulties with the 'scientific' inaccuracies of our forbears. Their faith was reinforced by the stories in these carvings. I doubt that any one individual can ever savour all the nuances of the thoughts that inspired them. In one sense this does not matter so long as we do not deny that they made the carvings with love and care and a desire to express a devotional thought. Even if we do not understand we must not belittle the record they left for us. It fascinates and draws us to investigate more closely. This book may help us to comprehend a tiny part of what there is to see and of the spiritual imagery that filled their lives. The extraordinary fact is that it can be as relevant and fresh for us today as it was when first created.

BIBLIOGRAPHY & REFERENCES

1   Anderson, M.D.
    Animal Carvings in British Churches.
    C.U.P. 1938

2   Anderson, M.D.
    The Medieval Carver.
    C.U.P. 1935.

3   Anderson, M.D.
    The Imagery of British Churches.
    John Murray 1955

4   Anderson, M.D.
    Drama and Imagery in English Medieval Churches.
    C.U.P. 1963.

5   Anderson, M.D.
    The Saint at Stake.
    C.U.P. 1964.

6   Anderson, M.D.
    History and Imagery in British Churches.
    John Murray 1971.

7   Anderson, W & Hicks, C.
    Green Man.
    Harper Collins London and San Francisco 1990

8   Barber. R.
    Bestiary. English version of the Bodleian M.S. 764.
    Folio Soc. 1992.

9   Barber, R.
    The Arthurian Legends.
    Boydell Press 1979.

10 Beigbeder. O.
    Lexique des Symboles
    Zodiaque.L.P.Q.V. 2nd Ed 1989.

11 Bernheimer, R.
    Wild Men in the Middle Ages.
    Harvard Univ. Press. 1952.

12 Bloomfield Morton W.
    The Seven Deadly Sins.
    Michigan. State College Press. 1952.

13 Camille Michael.
    The Gothic Idol.
    C.U.P. 1989.

14 Carter, Dagny.
    The Symbol of the Beast.
    N.Y. 1957.

15 Cave. J.P.
    Roof Bosses in Medieval Churches.
    C.U.P. 1966.

16 Charbonneau - Lassay, Louis.
    The Bestiary of Christ.
    Trans . D.M.Dooling. Arkana Books. 1992.

17 Clark, Willene B. & McMunn, Meradith T.
    Beasts & Birds of the Middle Ages.
    Philadelphia. 1989.

18 Collins, Arthur H.
    Symbolism of Animals & Birds represented in English Church Architecture.
    London 1913

19 Collins, Arthur H.
    Some Twentieth Cent. Animal carvings & their sources in the Bestiaries.
    Connoisseur. 1940. vol 106. pp238-243.

20 Cooper, J.C.
    An Illustrated Encyclopaedia of Traditional Symbols.
    Thames & Hudson. 1978.

21 Curley. Michael J.
    Physiologus.
    Univ. Texas, Austin & London.

22 Debidour, V.H.
    Le Bestiaire Sculpté en France.
    Arthaud. 1961

23 Druce. G.C.
    The Bestiary of Guillaume Le Clerk.
    Trans by. Printed for private Circulation .
    Headly Bros.1936.

24 Druce. G.C.
    The Medieval Bestiaries & their influence on Ecclesiastical & Decorative art.
    Archaeological Journal. Dec 1919 pp40-82.

25 Druce. G.C.
    The symbolism of the Crocodile in Middle Ages.
    Archaeological Jnl. 1909. pp310-338

26 Druce. G.C.
    The Amphisbaena & its connections in Ecclesiastical art & Architecture.
    Archaeological Jnl. VolLXVII 1910

27 Druce. G.C.
    The Elephant in Medieval Legend & Art.
    Archaeological Jnl. Vol LXXVII p 1-73

28 Druce. G.C.
    Queen Camel Church. Bosses on the Chancel Roof.
    Somerset Archaeological
    & Natural History Soc. vol LXII

29 Druce. G.C.
    Legend of Serra or Sawfish.
    Proc. Soc. of Antiquaries.
    VolXXXI 1918. pp20-35

30 Foster, R.
    Patterns of Thought.
    London 1991

31 Friedman, J.B.
The Monstrous Races in Medieval Art & Thought.
Harvard 1981.

32 Gardner.A.
Minor English Wood Sculpture.
Tiranti. London. 1958.

33 Hassig, Debra.
Medieval Bestiaries. Text, Image and Ideology.
Camb. Univ. Press. 1995

34 George, Wilma & Brunsdon Yapp.
The Naming of Beasts.
Duckworth London. 1991.

35 Hicks, Carola.
Animals in Early Medieval Art.
Edinburgh Univ. Press.1993.

36 James. M.R.
The Bestiary.
L 1 426 in Camb Univ. Lib. Oxford
for the Roxburghe Club. 1921.

37 James. M.R.
The Apocryphal New Testament.
Oxf. 1924.

38 Jerman.J. & Weir.A.
Images of Lust.
Batsford 1986.

39 Keyser.C.E.
Norman Tympana and Lintels. 2nd Edn.
Elliott Stock. London. 1927.

40 Klingender.F.
*Animals in Art & Thought to the end
of the Middle Ages.*
London 1971.

41 Maccoll. D.S.
Grania in Church; or the Clever Daughter.
Burlington Magazine. 8. 1905.pp80-86.

42 Mâle.E.
Religious Art in France. 12th Century.
Princeton Univ. Press. 1978.

43 Mâle.E.
Religious Art in France 13th Century.
Princeton Univ. Press. 1984.

44 McCulloch, Florence.
Medieval Latin and French Bestiaries.
Chapel Hill 1962.

45 Metford, J.C.J.
Dictionary of Christian Lore & Legend.
Thames & Hudson. 1983.

46 Mode. H.
Fabulous Beasts and Demons.
Phaidon. 1975.

47 O.E.D.
Compact Oxford English Dictionary.
O.U.P.1991.

48 Osterwijk, Sophie.
!4thc. Sculptures in aisle walls of York Minster.
York Historian.9.1990.2-16.

49 Owst. G.R.
Literature & Pulpit in Medieval England.
Blackwell .Oxf. 1961.

50 Randall. Lilian M.C.
Images in the Margins of Gothic Manuscripts.
Univ. Calif. Press. 1966.

51 Randall. Lilian M.C.
The Snail in Gothic Marginal Warfare.
Speculum. 1962. Vol.XXXVII pp358-367.

52 Romilly Allen. J.
Norman Sculpture & the Medieval Bestiaries.
Rhind lectures in Archaeology. 1885. Pub 1887.

53 Rowland. Beryl.
Animals with Human Faces.
A Guide to Animal Symbolism.
London 1973.

54 Smith.J.C.D.
A Guide to Church Woodcarvings.
David & Charles. 1974

55 Smith.J.C.D.
Church woodcarvings. A West Country Study.
David & Charles. 1969.

56 Speculum Humanae Salvationis.

57 Voraigne, Jacobus de.
The Golden Legend.
Trans. William.G.Ryan.
Princeton Univ. Press 1993.

58 White.T.H.
The Book of Beasts.
Translation from a Latin Bestiary of 12th C.
London.

59 Wildridge, T.Tindall.
The Grotesque in Church Art.
London 1899.

60 Wittkower. R.
Marvels of the East.
Journal of Warburg & Courtauld Inst.
V. 1942 p160ff, re Pygmies.

61 Wittkower. R.
Jnl of the Warburg & Courtauld Inst.
II. 1938-39. pp293-328

62 Wood. Rita.
The Romanesque Doorways of Yorkshire, etc.
Yorkshire Archaeological Jnl.
Vol 66. 1994. pp59-90.

63 Wright, T.
*Popular Treatises on Science written in the Middle
Ages in Anglo Saxon, Anglo Norman and English.
Includes Lives of Creatures by Phillipe de Thaun 1121*
Historical Soc. of Science . MDCCCXLI.

64 Young. Brian.
The Villein's Bible.
Barrie & Jenkins. London. 1990.

65 Zarnecki. G.
English Romanesque Sculpture 1060 - 1140.
London 1957.

66 Zarnecki. G.
Later English Romanesque Sculpture 1140 - 1210.
London 1953

INDEX excluding places.

M

N

O

P

Q

R

S

INDEX of places with photographs in the text.